GRAY DIVORCE STORIES

The Truth About Getting Divorced Over 50
From Men and Women Who've Done It

By

Barry Gold

D1124791

For Daniel and Andrew. The marriage may not have gone the distance, but Mom and I made you two, which means it was a smashing success.

Table of Contents

Introduction

Gray Divorce is booming in the United States.

The best study of the topic, "The Gray Divorce Revolution" by sociologists Susan Brown and I-Fen Lin, says that between 1990 and 2010 the divorce rate among Over 50's doubled, while it declined in every other demographic. In 1990, one out of ten Americans experiencing divorce was over 50. Twenty years later it was one out of four. Over 600,000 people over 50 got divorced in 2010.

Though it's unfortunate a more recent study hasn't been presented, common sense and anecdotal evidence suggest the numbers have continued to rise.

Another thing common sense and anecdotal evidence suggest: With so many Baby Boomers actually getting divorced, a huge number must be considering it. Many, many less-than-happily-married over 50's must be asking themselves, Does a divorce make sense for me?

We call these folks Divorce Curious, or in internet-speak, "Di-Curious."

Any person going through a Gray Divorce, or considering one, is desperate for information.

If you're in the process, you want to know if your experience is typical, how long certain feelings will last, what you need to do to recover, what your future may hold, and so much more.

And if you're Di-Curious, you want all the information you can gather to help you answer The One Overriding Question: Will I be better off if I get out?

One good resource is friends or family members who've been through a divorce. Maybe you have a few candidates you could reach out to. Of course, since you know each other, they may not be comfortable speaking with complete candor. They may not be telling you the whole story, in an effort to protect themselves or their spouse.

But that's okay, because now you've got this book. It's as if you have eighteen men and women who are as close as friends or family members, but who have no reason to hold anything back. They will tell you their complete stories – the good, the bad, and the ugly. You'll hear it all about their marriages, their Gray Divorces, and their recoveries. And perhaps the most important thing you'll learn is you're not the only one feeling this way. So many other people are experiencing some of the same things you are.

These people are telling their stories because they responded to a post on my website, DivorcedOver50.com, seeking volunteers to be interviewed about their experiences. They were promised anonymity; all names have been changed, as well as other identifiable facts. The interviews all took place over the phone, were recorded, transcribed, then edited for clarity and story-flow.

But in every case, you'll be reading an individual's story, told the way he or she chose to tell it, in his or her own words.

The interviewees live in all parts of the United States, with one Canadian in the mix. A few live in huge cities, others in smaller towns. For some, their divorces are not yet final, one has been divorced for a dozen years, and everyone else falls somewhere in between.

Chances are good you'll find at least a few of these stories very relatable, with similarities to your own situation. You'll probably like some of the respondents, and dislike others. You'll have sympathy for many, disdain for a few.

But every story presents an opportunity to learn something that could be valuable to you. For example, one woman found yoga to be a great help during her divorce. Another woman learned to be aggressive doing online dating. And another found relief by considering her ex to be a Dead Man (considering him that, not making him so…).

There are some themes. Many people speak of the pain of grieving their divorce, though acknowledging it's an important part of moving on. On a more pleasant note, you'll hear several women comment that their sexuality has reignited after their divorce, finding themselves pleasantly surprised to be having the best sex of their lives.

And hey, let's call a spade a spade: It's just plain interesting to hear about the private things that go in other people's lives.

The respondents were overwhelming female; men accounted for less than a quarter of the stories. Does that mean women are more open to discussing this topic than men? Possibly. But it could also mean more women use the site, and thus saw the post. There's no way to know.

But it really doesn't matter since so many divorce experiences and emotions are gender-neutral. Men can certainly learn from reading the women's stories, and vice versa. Additionally, it's a chance to gain some insight into the thinking and viewpoint of the opposite sex, which is not only good to know generally, but could be helpful for anyone who wants to resume dating.

Please remember that the interview subjects chose to tell their stories, which may account for the high percentage that have fairly happy endings. Or it may not.

These interviews are presented for their informational value. This book is not intended to advocate for divorce.

Rather, as you can see at DivorcedOver50.com, we put forth the following philosophy about gray divorce: It isn't ideal, and it wasn't the plan. Divorce should never be taken lightly, and it's never easy. But it can provide an opportunity to start over, hit the reset button, and get back to being who you want to be, as you move forward into a happy, fulfilling, and brighter future.

No matter the path you're on, or the one you choose, I wish you good luck on your journey.

Barry Gold
We welcome you to join our community at DivorcedOver50.com

Donna: It's Terrifying, But You Can Do It

Donna's in her early fifties. She was married just under twenty years. In hindsight, she missed plenty of red flags about her husband. When her children were little, Donna felt like a single mother, working full time and being their primary caregiver. Switching to a stay-at-home role didn't suit her either. She began to freelance, quickly building her business. Being busy made her feel good, and it allowed her time away from her husband. A final stab at therapy proved fruitless, so she filed for divorce. Since then, she's encountered so many men and women who are unhappy in their marriages, and are seeking guidance. Her advice: It's the most terrifying thing you'll ever do in your life, and financially you'll probably get hurt. But you can do it.

I never had that stereotypical attitude of so many girls: Ooh, I can't wait to get married. I figured I'd just wait and see what happens. I had a lot of fun in my twenties. And I enjoyed dating. And having disposable income, and all that stuff.

But in my late twenties, I knew I wanted to have a family one day. I was looking for someone who was very honest, and loyal, and all those really solid things.

We got introduced by a mutual friend. We were living in two different towns, so we dated long distance. This was before cell phones, so we'd talk on the regular phone once or twice a week. And we'd see each other on weekends. And he was a solid guy, so that was very attractive to me.

We dated for quite a while, and then at some point I was ready to say, You know what, I'm going to start dating around. But he proposed to me, and I said yes.

There were a lot of red flags that I should have paid attention to, but I didn't. Because I just didn't. I didn't know any better, I guess.

For instance, we went on this pre-marriage retreat that his church ran. They had these group exercises, where we'd talk about certain topics. The very last activity was to go away individually and write a love letter to our future spouse. I took it very seriously, pouring my heart and soul out. But when we got together to read each other our letters, he didn't have one. He couldn't do the assignment. He got stuck. And he was so stressed out about it. He said he just couldn't do it, but he would.

He never did. Helloooo….

It was a very early sign of his inability to not only know how he felt, but to share his feelings on a deep level. But at the time, I was so understanding — he's not a writer, it's hard for him, etcetera.

I would describe our marriage as very comfortable. Our sex life was nothing to write home about, but it was nice. So it was a very pleasant existence. I thought this was what marriage was supposed to be.

I continued to work full time through the births of both my children. His job required a lot of travel. So here I was, working full time, being the primary caregiver, everything. And then also not sleeping very much. I had the kids at daycare at 7:00am, then I'd go to work, I'd come home, and sometimes I even needed a babysitter because I had evening functions.

I was manic. I was sleep-deprived. Something had to give. We decided I'd stay home, because he made more money. I never thought I'd be a stay-at-home-mom. That wasn't my thing. But I thought this was the best way to go.

In many ways I was a single mom. That didn't help the marriage.

When the kids were in middle school, it began to bubble to the surface that I wasn't happy. I attributed it to the fact that I was fully doing the mom thing.

So I began to freelance. And things began to go pretty well. It gave me a life back. I thought that had solved the problem.

But we still weren't having deep conversations at home. I didn't have any intimacy — that personal connection with

Gray Divorce Stories

somebody. I tried so hard. I started realizing that all those red flags, the not being able to express himself, were really present. It took some time, but finally I realized that the marriage was in trouble.

If you would have asked him, he would have said everything was awesome. I was literally doing everything, other than maybe mowing the lawn. I look back and think, What the hell? I was a one woman show. And I didn't even realize it at the time.

When the economy crashed, they cut down on his travel. Now we're under the same roof, every day. And that was awful. It started going downhill fast after that.

I would tell him I was unhappy, and we'd have really good talks, seemingly, but then the next day it was like we had never spoken. I enabled him. I admit my part in it, as I later learned in therapy. I should have, years ago, said this is a deal breaker. And we have to fix this. But I didn't.

I began to get more opportunities to freelance, and I immersed myself in them. It was a distraction. I was really busy. I welcomed it, because it made me feel good. I felt viable again. Oh my, here's the person that I was. But I also used it, not knowingly, as a way to be gone a lot. Especially when he was home.

As I became more visible in the community, I had a lot of men approach me. Or want to talk to me. I was very good at pushing them away. But, I enjoyed it. Oooh, what is wrong with this picture? I could have easily had an affair. But I didn't.

I used to be real judgmental about things like that. But now I understand. People get so miserable in their marriages. I understand why it happens.

Around this time I was admitting I was unhappy. I had asked him to go to a counselor. He kept delaying, and we kept living our separate lives.

Finally, we went to therapy. But I knew the very first day that it wasn't going to work out. I started crying. But I gave it the college try. We started in the fall, but by spring it wasn't going well, and I said, I can't do this anymore. This is over.

We started the divorce process. It became real. We chose to do mediation. I believed that would be the most humane way to go. I said, Do you want to look at a place, or do I have to? And he said I had to move out. So I did.

I moved out with barely anything. It was terrifying. And he made it excruciating and difficult every step of the way. A side of him that very few have seen came out. He made it hard to get a dime.

I found a place, I moved out, started from scratch.

We went through an horrible mediation process that lasted much longer than it should have. It was just awful. He was uncooperative and just mean.

The kids don't like being with him. They love being with me. They have never expressed regret that we split up, or wish that we got back together.

My teenage daughter is incredibly intuitive. He treats her the same way he treated me — there's a distance, an inability to connect, an inability to have deep conversations. She doesn't feel cherished or loved. He's very stunted emotionally. I covered for him for a lot of years. I enabled him in many, many ways. So now my kids are seeing the real him, just like I finally saw the real him.

As far as dating, one of my fears is overthinking things. I know that I need to just have fun for a while. But I also don't want to waste my time with somebody who's not even close to what I would want or need.

The whole thought of meeting somebody, who I'm not at all enjoying talking to — I'd rather take a hot bath and read a good book.

I tend to be a little bit on guard. Because there are a lot of weirdos out there. I guess I'm a little gun shy. I really would love to meet somebody and be friends with them first.

Sex during my marriage was always sweet and comfortable, but I'm a really passionate person. It wasn't that way with him. It was never great. And it became more infrequent. By the time we got into counseling, we were going on two years since we'd had sex. He would initiate, but I just couldn't do it. I wasn't connected with him.

I'm freaked out about the idea of online dating. A girlfriend said, Be prepared to see full frontal naked pictures of men. And I went, What? My hairdresser said her clients come in all the time saying men send them naked pictures. Are you serious? That is not what I'm looking for.

I'm not built for one night stands. I can control that, obviously, but I don't even want to deal with somebody who thinks that's going to be a possibility.

I want intelligence, wit, and sense of humor. If you don't have those, then we're not going to meet for coffee. I guess I'll find that out if we talk on the phone.

One man that I did date a little — we never had sex, but we fooled around enough. And I am going to be so ready to go when the right guy comes along. Whoever that is will be getting some prize. I cannot wait, because I'm totally charged up sexually. I have a lot of time to make up for. I feel it. I know. I am ready to rumble. Oh yeah…

You'd think maybe my sex drive would be kind of low, but it's not. And what I'm finding out, from talking to friends, is that a lot of women my age are like, Whoo-hoo, let's go!

When I was young, my mother literally told me that old line about men not buying the cow when they can get the milk for free. I think that held me back. I didn't want to be too sexual, because that may be the only reason a man would like me.

And now, that's not an issue. I'm not looking for anybody to be a father to my children.

I've had so many women contact me, who wanted to talk about my experience, because they're miserable in their marriages, and do not know what to do.

And the element that's different with most women is the finances. That's the thing that stops most women from leaving. It's terrifying. I know women who are miserable in their marriages, but they will not leave. Because they are scared to death about how they'll live.

I was at the point where I didn't care if I lived in a tent. I knew I'd land on my feet.

When I went to rent my place, it was humiliating — I didn't have a pay stub to show I could afford it. I had to get my sister to co-sign on the lease. It was humiliating to be that age and not able to rent my own apartment.

There are so many people who aren't divorced, but are miserable, and cohabiting. And they will stay that way forever. It astounds me. Once I started talking about it, friends would confide in me, tell me things like, We haven't had sex in five years. We're waiting for the kids to graduate.

It is a phenomenon. And I want to help women find the courage to do it. They need to know what they have in savings. And in both retirement plans. And they need to know what their state laws are. If it's no-fault, they are rightfully entitled to half.

It's the most terrifying thing you'll ever do in your life, and financially you probably will get hurt. But you can do it.

You're going to find yourself on the floor sobbing. You're going to feel like a complete loser some nights.

But that's okay.

Linda: Pieces of Me

Linda was married for 26 years. Money was always a problem, as her husband insisted on living above their means to impress friends and colleagues. There were also difficulties with his mother. The biggest issue, however, was communication. She wanted to discuss things, but he'd just say, It happened, get over it. Tired of being miserable, Linda got out. When friends offered condolences on her divorce, she told them it was something to celebrate. Among the positives: she's been kissed better than she had in the last 30 years, and reignited her sexuality. Most importantly, Linda felt she had given away the pieces of herself during her marriage; now, however, she's gotten them back and is dedicated to never giving them away again.

My now ex-husband and I actually went to high school together. We dated one time, but nothing came of it. When I moved back home after college, a friend asked if I'd go out on a double date with him, her, and her boyfriend. I remembered him being a nice guy, so I said sure.

So we did that date, and got comfortable fairly quickly. We were on and off a few times, but eventually it was going well, and we began living together.

One day I came home and asked him to marry me. I was 23. It was wonderful. I remember being in love, and just thinking it was the greatest thing.

It soon became clear, though, that my husband was a very impatient person. I'm not saying that's bad or good, it's just who he is. He wanted to have children right away. And I thought, Oh, I can do this. After all, our generation was taught we can do it all. We could work, have kids, we could keep the house. We could be Martha Stewart.

And so, six months in, I got pregnant.

Which kicked off a huge problem in our marriage: his mother. She clearly didn't like me, but then, when she learned I was pregnant, she wanted me to have an abortion. She said, You don't need kids. I was really dumbfounded, but I remember thinking, I don't recall us having to ask your permission.

I didn't tell my husband this, or any of the stuff with her.

That was the start, in all honesty, of the demise of our relationship. She was a thorn from the very beginning.

I took 15 years of her insults, and nastiness, until I finally told my husband he had to talk to his mom. He doesn't like conflict and confrontation. But he did go talk to her.

But then he completely checked out afterwards. That was 15 years ago.

We should have divorced ten years ago. Truly. There was an incident at a dinner with one of our children. And I can't even remember what he said specifically, but I do remember my jaw hitting the table. I still remember how hurt I felt, if not what he said exactly.

The one thing we never did well was communicate our feelings. I always felt like I had to swallow my feelings just because of all the stuff with his mom.

I was constantly crying my eyes out. I'd lay beside him every night and cry quietly. Or go into the living room and cry. I didn't want him to know.

I thought I was handling it okay, but I hadn't fooled anybody but myself. Anytime I spoke up about what I wanted in the marriage, my husband would just get nasty.

I still thought it could be better. We did try counseling, but that honestly made it worse. The therapist ended up firing us.

The next year he rented an apartment behind my back. He finally told me, but then he never even moved into it.

So he stayed around, and I have no doubt that our issues contributed to some very serious problems for our younger child.

I was suffering migraines. But I thought it was easier to just go along with stuff. It wasn't worth the struggle.

As for our sex life, I truly felt like it was just a habit. He's the man, who needed a release. But there was no cuddling, no pillow talk. No real intimacy, for years. I would ask him to take me out, since I was home with the kids all day. But he'd say no, he was out all the time, and didn't want to do that. So I'd get to make dinner. I never got to dress up.

Another problem we had was with money. Or, really, he had the problem with money. He had to belong to the country club, or buy other things we could not afford.

He wanted me to be a stay-at-home mom because that made him look better. When I'd suggest going back to work, he'd say, So-and-So's wife doesn't work, so I don't want you to work. Like he's doing so well his wife doesn't have to work. But we needed the money. So I started working a little, but he hated it. He tried to talk me out of it. He made it seem like my work was pointless.

He's good at what he does, and makes very good money. But he has to live like he makes more. We always had to buy a home in a certain neighborhood, because So-and-So lives there. Not because we could afford it. When we finally sold the house after the divorce, it had three mortgages. So I didn't get anything out of it.

A couple years ago, I went back to work more steadily, getting a part-time job. I got my own checking account — which he hated. But I enjoyed it because I could buy the kids the things I wanted to without having to worry. It also gave me control of my money. He wanted it in a joint checking account. But I knew if I put it in there, I'd never see any of it.

So that really festered in him.

Going back to work, and making my own money, really helped me. I would put a little, and sometimes a lot, of money into the joint account, and he promised he'd pay me back, but he never did.

And finally, I was just so unhappy I moved forward with a divorce. You have to have someone willing to communicate and work through the issues. But I married a man who would say, Oh, just get over it. It happened, just move past it. That's a lot of what I got.

In my state, there's a waiting period before your divorce is final. I know the exact day. And then I'm having a freedom party.

I have friends who hear we're divorcing. And they say, I'm sorry. And I say No, don't be sorry. This is a good thing. This is such a good thing. I can breathe.

I truly wanted my marriage to be one of those sixty to seventy year marriages. I don't know if my desire was so strong that it blinded me to everything else.

My ex-husband is not the man I fell in love with. I see a picture of him that my daughter posted on Facebook, and those aren't the eyes of the man I fell in love with.

I do read a lot about divorce and the next phase. That's let me know what I'm thinking and feeling is okay. And it's normal.

I see it as a wonderful opportunity.

You know, this "'til death do you part" stuff was written when people died in their thirties or forties.

I have another lifetime. Do I want to spend that next lifetime miserable? Like I spent the last seven, eight, or nine years? No. I am looking forward to meeting someone new, and having that pillow talk. I asked my ex for thirty years to walk with me, and he never would. I want someone who wants to walk, hike, kayak. And that's exciting. It is an opportunity to go out in a blaze.

Friends of mine encouraged me to try online dating. I thought, How am I going to find a relationship online? They continued to needle me, and I finally went to a site for people over 50. It's a paid site, because I thought maybe there'd be a better quality of person on it, as much as I hate to say that.

I met a man a few months ago, and he's a sweetheart. He was the very first one I talked to. I was such a nervous wreck. I was so scared, I even used a bogus name. But we started talking, and he said, I'd love to meet you. And I'm like, How do I do this?

We did meet for a cup of coffee. The next night we went to dinner.

I'm surprisingly attracted to him. I asked my counselor if I should feel guilty, but she said, No, you've been alone so long, you want someone to hold you.

The kissing is awesome. His kisses are so tender. And I'm like, Wow, I don't remember this. I'm sure 30 years ago it was like that, but I just haven't been kissed so sweetly in such a long time.

He's about a year ahead in his journey. So he's dated a bit. And he's looking for a commitment. I'm not dating anyone else, but I can't give a commitment now. He's a super nice guy. He's three years younger. He constantly calls me a Cougar.

We went out for a couple months, and just went away together for the first time recently. I was so nervous, it was like losing my virginity all over again. But he was so receptive to conversation and communication. That's a huge factor for me. I told him, This is going to be like the first time all over again. I'm older, things are different. I don't know how my body is going to respond to someone else. And he said, I think it'll be okay.

And it was wonderful. He knows how a woman's body responds, and he was caring, and gentle, and tender, and WOW!

I thought I was going to wait, but it just happened. And it happened at the right time.

I've read articles about being divorced, and sex at this age, which say it's okay to have one night stands — which I wouldn't do. But they say just make sure you're psychologically ready for whatever you do.

I love being by myself. I love my own company. But I still want to spoon with a warm body. I want him kissing my neck. So he'll be staying over here, too.

I think sex now is very freeing. I enjoyed it. And I think part of that is I don't have kids to worry about, in the back of my brain. Are they asleep? Do they need to eat? Without that, I can relax and get into it more.

I don't think that with someone else it would have been as sweet. He was so patient and understanding. And he listened, and he talked with me about it.

I refuse to pigeonhole men based on my ex-husband. I've seen some good men out there. And that's what I want.

I don't want to get married, but I do want to be with someone.

I think when you look too hard for something, you miss what's right under your nose. You can miss the right thing.

The guy I'm with, I'm attracted to him, but I had this voice inside saying he's not my type. But then I realized, I have to stop that. I don't want to lose this guy. He's been an absolute charm to me. Not my type? What does that mean?

I'm thrilled. I don't begrudge any of it. I don't harbor any ill will or anger toward my ex. It's part of the journey. What I've done through this is find "me" again. The pieces of me I gave away over the years — I've gotten all those pieces back. And I don't know that I could have done it any other way.

But it's made me resolve to never lose my pieces again.

Mindy: It Was Not My Dream

Mindy is in her mid-fifties. Her marriage was difficult from the get-go, with a husband who was abusive and possibly bi-polar. She tried to keep her marital problems at bay by staying busy, homeschooling her children while also running a business. But finally her husband's erratic behavior, for which he refused to seek help, became too much. She divorced him for the good of herself and her children, yet continued to shield her kids from details about their dad. She's taking it slow as a single woman, more interested in friendships than romance. And while a number of her unhappily married acquaintances envy her situation, she counsels them that divorce is difficult and painful.

I met my husband at community college, on the first day of my first class, American Lit. He was older. He'd been a hippie guy, traveling, doing his thing. He had started school, then been married and divorced. And had come back to finish up.

So here I was, twenty years old, off at college, meeting an older man. We hit it off well, and started dating.

I was very innocent. Very sheltered. I was also kind of a smart ass. So I came off as being more worldly than I actually was. I think he liked that I was young and cute and whatever.

We dated for a while. He graduated. He moved. I came along for a summer. But things were not going well. I went back to school, convinced I'd start a new life.

And he followed me back down there.

And not too long after that, I got pregnant. I had almost finished school, but now I had a baby.

He wanted to get married, but I wouldn't actually marry him right away.

I said, Look, I don't want you to marry me just because we have a kid together. I want you to marry me because you want to be married to me. Which, to this day, is the reason I think we made it as long as we did.

So we did get married, and proceeded to have three more children together.

We were great as parents. As a couple, not so much. It was a problematic marriage from the get-go.

I think things really started to deteriorate about six years ago. Like a lot of people, I tried to wait it out until the kids were out of the house.

There was a fair amount of abuse in the relationship, so that was obviously problematic as well.

It was cyclical. Things would go well for several months, and then he'd kind of have a meltdown. He may be bi-polar. He never would go to get help. I put up with it.

I threw myself into the kids. I homeschooled them through high school. And had another business. I was super busy. As long as I kept active, the other problems were secondary.

But about three years ago I sat him down and said, Look, if you want to stay married to me, I need you to get some counseling.

He was spiraling out of control. Not paying bills. Being dishonest. I needed to be able to trust him. And for him to address some of his emotional issues.

I loved him. I didn't want to divorce him. But I knew I couldn't live like that.

He said, Oh yes, I'll certainly do those things. But he didn't. He didn't do anything.

His mentality was very stoic. He could deal with things. He was not going to ask for help. Which is okay, except when it affects the people you love and care about. Or should love and care about enough to address your issues.

I just got to the point where I said, I'm sorry, I can't do this anymore. So finally I took the steps to start a divorce.

And it was horrible. Awful. Hideous.

I sat him down to tell him. We met at a coffee shop. We had this huge blow out. And he was very angry. I said, Look, we've been good parents through all of this. Let's try to be good parents through the divorce. I'm not looking to hurt you. I care for you. I love you. But I don't want to be your wife anymore. I just can't. And I moved out.

The biggest problem is he's not following through on commitments to our two youngest kids. I don't care about me, but it's really hurting the two of them.

My son came up to me and said, You know, Mom, when you first left Dad, I was really angry with you. But now I understand. I can see why.

On the one hand that's great. You're vindicated for leaving, you're not carrying all that guilt. On the other hand, it really hurts my heart because they're seeing a side of their father they were insulated from for a long time. So that's hard.

I knew that eventually the kids would see what I'm seeing. You love your kids, and you know they love their dad, but it's hard to defend the guy you're divorcing. I tried. I wasn't perfect, since I was so mad at him. But I did my best.

I didn't want the kids to go through what I went through, with their parents getting divorced when they were in their late teens. But in the end, he was getting so erratic and violent that I couldn't rationalize it to myself. So I had to do it.

My daughter initially planned to stay at home with her dad. I wasn't going to demand that she come. I just told her I had an extra bedroom available for her. Within a couple of weeks, she moved in with me. I told her she could still spend time with her dad. But she said, Nope.

I didn't want to be the kind of parent who turned a child against their dad. I want them to still have a relationship with him. I actually encouraged her to go to counseling. I thought it was important to work through these issues before she started dating, so she wouldn't take them with her always.

Emotionally, the younger two are having a rough time. But the older two are fine.

As for me, I'm not dating at all.

I've been a busy girl. I went back to school to finish my degree. I'm starting graduate school now. And I'm teaching at the university.

But I felt like, I don't want to date for a year. I want my divorce to be final. I want to give myself that time.

I know a lot of people, ten minutes after they separate they're trolling the bars. But that's not me. I just wanted to process everything.

I want to do it the right way. I want to do it mindfully. I'm not ready to do online dating. If somebody was interesting, I think I'd cultivate a friendship. Take a little more time before sleeping with the person.

I've heard of that "three-date rule" — if you don't want to have sex by the third date, the guy is out of there. I hope that's not the way it works. If that's his attitude, that's not somebody I want to be with.

When I was young, a big part of the attraction was, Is the guy going to be a good father? A good provider? And so forth. But at this point, it's more, Do I enjoy this person's company? Is this somebody I like spending time with? So there's a different perspective now.

It's really weird how people want to talk to you. One of my daughter's friends and her mom came over. When the girls scurried away, the mother and I were talking, just getting to know each other a bit. And the next thing I know, after I told her I was separated, she starts telling me she's not happy in her relationship. In these whispered tones. And I'm like, What am I supposed to say — That's unfortunate?

I was honest. I said, It's really hard. I would say, Think it through. Maybe consider getting counseling before you make a big move. Because it's very, very painful. Tough on me, tough on the kids.

One of my girlfriends, when I told her I was going back to school, said, You're living my dream. And I said, So your dream is to go through a horrible divorce and have your heart broken? If your dream is to go to school, then go to school. But it's not a package deal. You don't have to leave your husband and suffer and be miserable, and cry yourself to sleep for months at a time. If you're in a supportive relationship, you should be able to go to school anyway, if that's what you want to do.

Online dating is kind of intriguing. The idea of finding someone you have a lot in common with. But right now, the thought of going out on a date makes me feel ill. Not because I don't like men, I do. But just because I haven't done it since the eighties. It's kind of like, What?

Both of my daughters are giving me dating advice. The older one says, Mom, you can't just sit around. You've got to put yourself out there. But I'm really not ready for this yet. So she says that when I'm ready, she'll be there to shepherd me through.

I have looked at online sites. Some of the men are real gems. Some kinda look like serial killers. And I'm sorry, if you're going to post your picture on a dating site, comb your hair. And put a shirt on. I don't think anyone should take a selfie in the bathroom. Maybe I'm old school…

And I hear that people lie a lot. I would question a guy who says he's 5-10, but he's really 5-6. Not because someone 5-6 would be physically unappealing to me. It's that I'd think, Okay, if he's not honest about that, what else is he not going to be honest about? Maybe that's just a mom thing, or an older person thing.

I'm just looking to cultivate friendships at this point, particularly with men. I haven't interacted with adult men for years and years. It's gone pretty well — I've made some nice, non-romantic friendships.

I would think being a guy in your fifties or sixties would be fabulous. There are a lot more women out there looking, compared to when we were 25. For men in their fifties, there are going to be a lot of ladies checking them out. It should be sweet.

I definitely want to date somebody who's within five years, up or down, of me.

Many of my friends were married and divorced very young. And now they're on their second marriages, and doing well. Which kind of gives me hope.

I have found this bizarre, weird, situation where young guys, in their twenties, are trolling around. I'm like, Honey, no. This is not happening. You need to move on.

I'm not a stunning beauty or anything. It's not that I'm so gorgeous. I was talking to a friend, asking, Is this a mom thing? What's with these guys? You're at a restaurant, and you've got some young waiter flirting up a storm. I don't think they're just trying to get a better tip.

It's really been horribly confusing. If I was a size-one yoga master, or something, I would kind of get it. It's flattering the first couple of times. And then it started getting weird. There has to be something going on here that I'm not understanding.

I went to a divorce care class, and it was so sad. It was heartbreaking. There was one poor man, and fifteen women. And some of the women were ten years out from their divorce and just bawling like it happened a month ago. And I thought, You know, you need to move on.

I went on some websites for women who were divorced, and they were all about female empowerment. You're a good person even though your husband left. And I was like, That's nauseating. A lot of them seemed to be saying, Now that your life is over, we can help you.

I like a site that is informational, but there's no lingering despair. A site that acknowledges that divorce hurts, it's not fun, but that you're going to be okay.

I have good and bad days. At this point I'm ready to just concentrate on my studies.

It was not my dream to be a fifty-year-old divorced woman. It was not in my playbook at all. But I feel like there's nowhere to go but up.

And, in a way, you get to be more selfish. I get to say, This is what I want. And this is what makes me happy.

Greg: I Feel Like a Schlub

Early fifties Greg had a very up and down marriage, including a yearlong separation a decade ago. The first time they split, he blamed it on himself — though she wanted to work on their issues, he's the one who pulled away. The second time, however, was the opposite, likely driven by his wife having a new lover. Though Greg had considered this possibility, he was really knocked off-kilter when it was confirmed. Greg's ego took a beating, as he wondered why she would rather make it work with someone new than try to fix things with him. Intellectually, Greg knows he's better off without a woman solely interested in herself, but it hurts to see she's moved on so easily while he continues to struggle.

I went to a singles' group event at a park, where I saw this beautiful blond. We played volleyball, and talked. It turned out we had the same favorite restaurant, which we went to on our first date.

We went out again, and that was it. We hit it off. She really liked me, and I really liked her. And we started spending a lot of time together.

She said she knew by the second date that I was the one.

We dated for nine months, then I proposed. And we got married nine months later. We bought a house a few years after that. It was good. For a while.

We had struggles. She had an issue that made it painful to have sex. She was dealing with that even before we got married. So sex was already starting to be a little difficult. I felt like I was hurting her. We couldn't even really have sex on our honeymoon. So it was rocky that way.

But other aspects were good. We had fun. We decided to start a family, and had two kids.

Though after having them, that's when things began to change.

It's the typical thing. You're taking care of the kids. You're taking care of things. You're taking care of everyday life. And I think I kind of turned off to her. I was feeling like she was not very giving.

Sex had become kind of like work. She was actually more into it than I was. But everything centered on her orgasm. The reason we were having it was so she could get off. I couldn't really talk about it with her. I'd make excuses not to do it. So she got really upset. And we just really drifted apart.

We had gone to see counselors on and off. It didn't seem to work too well. The years went on. We were unhappy. Just kind of like roommates.

About nine years ago we made the decision to split up. I moved out. We told the kids. They were both under ten. We were going to mediation. We were getting things done.

And then, the night before our last session with the mediator, we were at this dinner, and my wife said, Are we sure we're doing the right thing?

We started talking about it. And opened up. I was finally able to say all the things that I couldn't say before. And it brought out all of the things that reminded us of what had brought us together.

And that rekindled the spark.

We put off the last mediation meeting. We just started "seeing each other" again. Kind of dating. All of a sudden it was really exciting again. For the first time in a long time I had hope. It felt like we had figured it out.

We ended up getting back together. I moved back in after a year of being away.

In that year, I had maybe one or two dates. My wife, later, admitted that she'd had an affair before I'd moved out. And I'm pretty sure she was seeing somebody while we were apart.

After I moved back in, it was good for about a year. Maybe.

We both went to a therapist together. And I saw my own.

Then, one day, this person from her work called the house. And told me my wife was having an affair with someone at work. They said they saw it happening, and just had to tell me. They couldn't stand by and watch what she was doing to me.

So I confronted her with it. And she admitted it. I felt like a chump, but I forgave her.

Slowly, whatever magic we thought we had, just melted away. After two years it was back to the same as before.

But I felt kind of stuck. I had already left once. I couldn't sit down and tell my kids that we're going to do it again. I think we both felt stuck.

And then she went through menopause, so we didn't hardly have any sex in the last three years of our marriage. Maybe not even one time.

We'd go away on weekends, and it would seem to be better, but then we'd come home, and the reality would set in.

The difference is, the first time I was the one who turned off. I wouldn't make any effort to fix things, and pushed her away.

This time, it was the opposite. I wanted to figure it out. But she just totally turned off to me. All of a sudden, I'd kiss her, and it wouldn't be good, and eventually I lost confidence, like I didn't know what to do. I felt like nothing I did was any good. It just wasn't working.

So we were back to being roommates. We were running the house well. We were good parents. We had our finances in order. We'd gotten rid of all our debt. Everything was working, except the marriage.

I was willing to accept that it was not great, but it was not terrible. And she could be nice and fun, and every once in a while I got glimpses of the person who I fell in love with. But by that point she had shut herself off completely.

And then eighteen months ago we started talking about splitting. I had a feeling she may have met somebody again. She said, What are we doing? Are we going to just keep on this way?

We didn't have much in common anymore. We did everything apart. She was never shy about finding the time to pursue her interests. I didn't really have any interests except taking care of the kids. And taking care of the house. And taking care of business.

I assumed she met someone. And then she finally decided she didn't want to just play house anymore. She was done pretending like we're a happily married couple.

So we did the divorce, this time to completion.

Out of the twenty years we were married, about half of that time was not very good.

She called recently, panicked, saying we needed to talk. The last time she did that, she wanted to get back together. I wondered if that's what she wanted this time.

So we met. And she told me she was in a relationship, that she had a boyfriend. The urgency was that our son had run into them a couple of times. And he was all upset. He'd told her it wasn't fair that she hadn't told me. And threatened that if she didn't tell me, he would.

That really threw me for a loop. I hadn't thought it would. When I got out of the marriage, it was kind of a relief. It had been bad. You get out and feel like there's a lot of hope. She's moved out, I've got the place to myself. I don't have to deal with her anymore. And I can just think about me and the kids.

I had assumed she'd met somebody, but that didn't really bother me very much. Until it actually became concrete — that's when I started imagining her having the relationship with someone else that I wanted to have with her.

I feel like a blob and schlub, and she's with some guy who lifts weights and is in much better shape than me. A virile sexual partner, blah, blah, blah, that I'm not. I know that's just in my imagination, but that kind of threw me into a funk.

And then she went with him on the vacation that she and I were supposed to go on. We had reserved this place eighteen months earlier to use, and never cancelled. So she kept the date, but ended up going with her boyfriend.

It was supposed to be our romantic get-away to Hawaii — she went, just not with me. How selfish is that? She wouldn't want to try with me, but would rather move on to someone else?

She was never shy about doing what made her happy. I always characterized it as: I would get up every day thinking about how I could make her happy. And she would get up every day thinking about how I could make her happy.

I look back on the early days and I really get sad. There really was something there. It wasn't nothing. It wasn't my imagination.

But at the same time, nobody I knew, none of my friends, were surprised at all. They wondered how it had lasted so long. Nobody really liked her very much. Except for me.

We'd go out of town to visit my mother. And I'd do all the work, all the schlepping. Taking care of the kids. And she'd get up, do her own thing, go on walks. She was always very aloof and apart from everybody else. She was just concerned about herself. So it's nice not having to deal with that anymore.

When I found out she was in a relationship I felt like kind of a loser. So I thought maybe I'd try to do something also. I started online dating, and just absolutely hated it.

Putting the profile together was like writing my resume. It felt like when I was unemployed and looking for a job. Writing cover letters and not hearing back. It's like trying to sell yourself.

Online led to two coffee dates. But nothing happened.

My friend's girlfriend fixed me up with one of her friends. The four of us went for a drink. It was nice. And then just she and I got together. She's very nice, attractive. But I just felt nothing. I've just got nothing to talk to her about. Nice, but not stimulating.

I just don't know. I want to meet someone, but maybe I'm not ready. Whenever I make plans, I'm not looking forward to them, I'm almost dreading them. I guess that means I'm just not ready.

But how come it was so easy for her? To just find somebody, right away?

Can't he see that she's all about herself? She's the same person she was before. Is she somehow different with him than she was with me?

It could be that maybe she wasn't physically attracted to me anymore. And then she met someone who was much more of a turn on for her. A guy who sizzles all those juices that were not sizzling with me.

Maybe it was different perceptions. My perception was I was doing everything I could for her. And yet her perception was that I wasn't thinking of her. She would get mad at me for not doing what she expected me to do for her.

My best friend was way more unhappy in his marriage than me. And now he's with someone who's our age. And their sex is incredible. But I think maybe I'm not terribly attracted to fifty year old women.

I don't know what I'm looking for. I had lost hope. I feel like a schlub, and that I won't be attractive to anybody. Because she wasn't attracted to me. It's hard not to think that, especially when you're kind of prone to think like that already.

I think I'll just meet someone naturally, when I'm ready. Online seems so contrived. And difficult for me. Other people may love it. But for me, it's not right.

I just want to meet somebody who intellectually turns me on.

The problem is, I was never that good at dating before I got married. And now, to get back out there, that's scary.

Gayla: If My Ex Could See Me Now

Gayla is in her late fifties. Her marriage to her high school sweetheart was marked by horrible communication, and sex that felt like a chore. She poured herself in her children, slogging through until the oldest had graduated college. She found yoga to be a great salvation as she spent the first year after her split figuring out who she is, and what she wants. Then she began to date again, discovering a world of sexuality unlike anything she'd imagined. Though it was shocking at first, she threw herself into it completely, dating multiple men at the same time, as well as engaging in some non-traditional arrangements. But she stays safe, and sleeps home every night. As Gayla says, Life is pretty darn good.

I got married when I was 18.

He was my high school sweetheart, my first real boyfriend. We met when he was in grade ten, and I was in grade eleven. I was the oldest of three, and just kind of wanted to get out of the house.

I'd be mortified if my daughter decided to get married at eighteen. I don't know why my mother didn't say anything. But she didn't.

We lived in an apartment, then I convinced him we needed to buy a house. So we bought a house. And then I had my first baby when I was 24. The second followed when I was 29.

And that was, sort of the turning point, I think.

I was so much more involved with the kids than he ever was. I did all of their activities, doctors' appointments, and things at school. He was too busy working. I think that's when things started to unravel. But we just kind of hung in there, for the sake of the kids.

And suddenly years later, you find yourself, when they're almost to university, saying, What are we doing?

Communication was horrible in our marriage. We never talked. And when he'd get mad at me for something, he wouldn't

Gray Divorce Stories

speak to me for a week. And then he'd be horny, and he'd be like, okay, I think I'll make up with her now.

He'd do this over and over and over again. And it's like, Wait a minute, this isn't working. I'd like to talk about why you were so pissed off. Not just sweep it under the rug. But that was the cycle we went through.

I just immersed myself in the kids, and their activities.

He lived in the basement in our home for a good couple of years before he actually left. It was a financial thing, too. We wanted to get the kids through university.

The kids did drift in and out when they were in school. So they knew dad was living separately. They didn't talk about it at all.

He actually had a girlfriend. And I suspected for a little bit that he'd been cheating. But I sort of tolerated it.

I don't blame him for his girlfriend, for finding her. Things were over before that happened. I don't put any blame on her at all. He would not have been out there looking if things had been fine at home. I still talk to her, I see her at family events.

When my daughter finished university, that's when he moved out.

He was always a good provider. He took care of us that way, for sure.

We had to have a valuation of his business done. It was complicated. A lot of cash transactions. I saw that through my marriage, so I knew how much there was. And of course the business came back way less than its real value.

At one point we got tired of talking with our lawyers, so we said, Well let's go down to the local bar and hammer something out. So we did. I wanted to keep the house. And he made me a really decent offer. Like really super decent. And I'm trying not to smile, and he's going, You know, this is what I want. And I said, Okay, okay, where do I sign? So I signed.

And he went back to his lawyer, and the lawyer said, Are you nuts? Do you really want to do this? But because he hated his lawyer, he said, Of course I want to do this. So the lawyer let it all go and didn't bother to try to convince him otherwise.

So it all worked out that way. We just hammered it out over a couple of beers.

I never threatened to blow the whistle on his cash business – I just wasn't going to go down that road. I wanted to keep it as friendly as possible. And I think part of it was guilt on his part, too.

So I got divorced about six years ago. And a lot's been happening since.

Around the time things first went sour, I started practicing yoga. And I found great salvation in it. It was just exactly what I needed. I needed some time to figure out who I am, and what I wanted, and all that sort of stuff.

I wasn't in a big hurry to get out there and start dating again. So I took about a year or so, just exploring, doing what I wanted to do. I still had my kids coming and going, an open house sort of situation.

Then finally I went online. And I'm gonna write a book about that someday.

I've met some very interesting characters. All my still-married friends want to hear my stories. They want to live vicariously through me. I've met some interesting guys. Some not so interesting guys. A lot of them I'm still friends with.

What I'm finding is, most of these guys don't want anything serious. They were married thirty years, they had to give up half of everything, they don't want to do that again.

We come with so much more baggage now. I try not to let that interfere with whatever is going on, but it's sort of a part of who you are.

This is who I am. And if you don't like it, that's fine. I'm not wearing makeup for you, I'm not putting high heels on for you. I'm not changing who I am.

I don't regret any of it. I do feel like I missed out on a lot. And I wasn't happy for many years. And I just buried it. I just buried all those feelings.

And I buried my sexuality too, because I hated having sex with him. Oh god, it's Saturday night, he's gonna start rubbing my back again, and I'd pretend to be asleep. It was awful… And I thought, is this what sex is about? Like, really?

But I would just do it. Like, Hurry up, come on, are you done yet? And I guess eventually that wore on him. It was a chore, like vacuuming, and laundry, things I had to do in my marriage.

So that was pretty depressing.

But I've turned that around now. Maybe a little too much, if that's possible.

I am dating more than one guy. And I just had a two-and-a-half-year relationship with a guy. We just broke up. But we were never really together. It was more about sex than anything. It was a friends-with-benefits arrangement. And he totally opened my eyes, he shocked me actually, at first, like totally shocked me. I was like, People really do that?

He came into my life for a reason. He came in to teach me about my own sexuality and what's out there. To this day, I'm still shocked at what goes on in the world, from a sexual standpoint. I still try to wrap my head around all these different types of relationships. It's weird.

The traditional, you get married, you stay married — that's all gone these days.

People are into such different things now. And I was like, Okay, I'm not going to judge anybody. Whatever, but wow. Wow.

Like a different world. That's what I found online.

The oldest guy I've ever dated was 60. And that was stretching it a little bit.

Most of them are younger. I'm seeing a guy now who's 48. And he's married. He's in "The Lifestyle." It's a completely open relationship with his wife. And she has a friend who she sleeps with all the time. I have a hard time kind of wrapping my head around it all. How does this work? Where does this go? What if somebody's feelings get deeper than they should be?

I met a couple that wanted me to join them. Okay, whatever turns you guys on. It's weird to me, but okay.

If my ex had any idea how things have turned completely around for me…

I've tried different dating sites. I did e-Harmony. I filled out pages and pages of questions, and at the end, they say, What's your marital status? And I put Separated. And it went, No, sorry, you have to be divorced. And I was annoyed, since I'd spent all that time. So I just did it again, and lied.

I got this match one time, and it was someone I knew, we were friends years ago. I always liked him, so I decided to call him. We chat for a bit, I mention that his profile came up, and he tells me he hasn't been on that site in years. So that kind of put me off. What are they doing? Just leaving profiles up that aren't even active anymore? And suggesting matches like that?

And I think some are fake, too. I've heard that sites make fake profiles. GQ models, with these professionally written profiles. This guy's too good to be true. And then, just as your membership is starting to expire, somebody like that likes you. So they sucker you back in. It's just about more money, right? Oh, somebody was peeking at your profile. Or So-and-So likes you. Just to get more money out of you.

I've kept my profiles pretty much the same on the different sites. I'd switch my pictures up from time to time. I didn't put a lot of pictures, or a lot of information up either. I'm not going to pour my heart out to people I don't know. They get a brief synopsis about who I am. I was honest. I wouldn't lie about anything. Just a condensed version.

There are so many weirdos on the free sites. Guys like, Hey baby, I like older women. I was just, No thank you.

My daughter showed me Tinder, but oh my god, that's so shallow.

I've almost always waited for the man to contact me first. I have broken that rule occasionally, if somebody was really intriguing. But for the most part, I guess I'm a little old-fashioned. I figure the guy should make the first move.

One thing I've done a couple of times is meet men who didn't put pictures in their profile. Quite brave of me. One was a guy who told me he was overweight, that he looked like John Goodman. I told him, I don't care. I'm not shallow like that. You don't have to be six feet tall and muscular. We dated a little while, but he was starting his own business and had no money. I don't care about a lot of money, but you need some.

And the other guy was a successful businessman who didn't want to put his picture up online. I'm still actually seeing him.

Sometimes I think I get in a little over my head with all of these guys. I mean, I don't tell them about each other, obviously. But if someone asks, I'll be honest. Sometimes it comes up in conversation, sometimes it doesn't.

The one who's married, we went out on a double-date, his wife and her friend, and him and me. It was the weirdest thing, the four of us out together. His wife's friend actually lives with his girlfriend, but she has no idea what he's doing.

I figure as long as I'm having fun, and I'm being safe, and I'm not putting myself in any situation where I'm gonna have an ax murderer knocking at my door, that's fine. I do sleep home at night. I sleep alone. Safety is a big concern. And if there's a guy who doesn't make me feel comfortable, forget it. I don't need him.

My sexuality came back on its own. There were a few guys where it wasn't the greatest, but I weeded them out. It was all a learning experience for me.

I think for many women, their sexuality gets buried. You just suppress it for so long. But it's somewhere deep inside there. And it just takes the right person or the right circumstances to unleash it.

I do have an open mind. I just accept what they're offering, and go with it. Just going with the flow. The yoga really helped. It teaches you to just live in the moment. And to breathe, and not think about the past, and the future. Just live in the moment.

For your sex life, it's amazing if you can do that. You just block everything else out, and concentrate on the hands that are on your body, or whatever. It's amazing.

It's kind of the unspoken thing they don't talk about in yoga – the mind-body connection. You get very connected with your body. It's a little hippy-ish, but I've met a lot of amazing people, instructors. It can be eye-opening.

I'm a little overwhelmed sometimes because I think I let too many men into my life. But they're all here for a reason. I can take a little lesson from each of them. How I want to be treated, how I don't want to be treated. I'm not intentionally breaking hearts or putting notches on my bedpost — that's not me. I love being alone, too. I like having the whole bed to myself. So there are definite advantages.

I have my moments. I tell my friends, this guy named Loneliness comes to visit. I tell him, You're not wanted. Go away. Sometimes he leaves, sometimes he hangs around for a while. That doesn't happen often.

You have to feel all those feelings, you have to go through it all. Feel the good times and the bad times. It's how you get where you are now.

In hindsight, I don't think I should have stayed in my bad marriage so long, to get the kids out. I don't think they learned about healthy relationships. Sometimes I think I did them a bit of a disservice.

I'm not in love, living happily ever, but I'm very content.

Life is pretty darn good.

Wendy: The Performance Was Lacking

Wendy is in her early fifties. A successful corporate type, she constantly made allowances for her husband, a musician who struggled at his career. After having a second child, Wendy was exhausted from being both the mom and the breadwinner. And then her husband developed some serious sexual performance issues. She thought that if she could keep everyone else happy, she'd be happy. But she was at her breaking point. Feeling abandoned in every possible way, Wendy trudged on, planning to stick it out until her children left home. But then she met a man at a business conference…

I was three years out of college and on a fast track career-wise, working for a large company.

A neighbor introduced me to my husband. He was cute and charming and motivated. His career was on the rise. And we fell in love really quickly. It was very intoxicating.

I admired his drive, his ambition. I was intrigued. He was the complete opposite of me. My background was very "Beaver Cleaver-ish". I'd had a stable family life. He came from a volatile family, and he was kind of the black sheep. I think I was attracted to the way he was different from me.

We got engaged six months after we met, and married nine months after that.

I've always had a corporate job. And even back then I was the breadwinner. But he worked. He was not a lazy person. He'd get a gig here, a gig there. It could be very random.

We weren't sure about having children. The first ten years were very good. We were devoted to each other. And we had a lot of fun. We didn't do a lot of socializing with other people. It was basically just the two of us. It was all good.

In the late nineties, he wanted to move for his career. So we picked up and moved. And he actually did pretty well there. He was making a good middle-class living.

We had our first child when we'd been married about ten years. And then a second child about four years later.

If I had to say where things turned, it was clearly after the birth of our second child. It began to get a little "interesting." Two kids diverted my attention away from him. I was enjoying the companionship of the other moms in the neighborhood. I was making really good friends. Just leaning away from him a little bit.

At the same time, he began to experience some significant career frustrations. 9/11 had a big impact. The drumbeat was starting — he was really unhappy. I was just so focused on trying to keep everything going. At that time, I was becoming an even bigger breadwinner for the family. I was doing a lot of business travel.

I hired a nanny when the kids were little. I had them in pre-school from the time they were one, to make sure he had his creative time. He was not a stay-at-home husband by any stretch. I still did all of the mom things — birthday parties, teachers' gifts, all of it.

And then there began to be some pretty significant sexual performance issues on his part.

So there was a lot going on, and we didn't handle any of it well. I'm a horrifically low conflict person. I started doing what I've done my whole life, which is just be a pleaser. I thought that if I can just make sure everyone is happy, I'll be happy.

I kept stuffing everything in. We had very infrequent, awkward, conversations about the sexuality piece. And he just was not open at all to even talking about it or discussing it. And candidly, I just put it on the shelf. Which shocks me now — I really can't believe it.

So at this point, I'm happy and fulfilled in my work. I'm fulfilled in my motherhood. I've got friends. But he's just completely miserable. He decides we have to move again, for his work.

We were literally at the breaking point. I finally said, If you want to move, we can move. It was a last ditch effort.

So my kids, both under 10, left the home they were born in. I left everything I loved. We did not know one person in our new city.

I put my head down, I was working my ass off. Taking care of the kids. Trying to help him get his career on track.

Then the fantasy in my brain started: How could I get out? My plan was always to wait until my youngest graduated high school.

I never really talked about my marriage with people. I was very private. There were people who suspected, but I just kept it in. People would ask about him, but I was the master at diverting the subject back to them.

The financial burden was just getting worse. I would tell him, for two or three years, I can't keep doing this. I'm fastidious about debt. I started telling him, You've got to step up.

I remember saying, All I need is a thousand dollars a month. I'm coming up about that short. It's not a lot. Just help me. But there was no help.

And no sex, in like ten years. Nothing.

So I was financially abandoned, physically abandoned, sexually abandoned, emotionally abandoned.

And I kept planning my exit, thinking about how I could do it.

I'm in a male industry, and travel for work. But I never stopped in a bar. I never returned a glance. I never flirted. Nothing. I was friendly, people liked me, I was respected. But I was never open to anything.

Then, about eighteen months ago, I was at a conference. There were sessions in the morning, individual meetings in the afternoon, and hospitality events in the evening.

I ended up having a meeting with this fella at the conference. It was not his first rodeo. The conversation went from business to flirting in about five minutes. And I went for it.

I told him about the problems I was having. He told me how he'd waited for his youngest child to leave for college, then had gotten out of his marriage. I told him how I was waiting to do the same.

And he said, So what do you do, have affairs? I almost fell over. I said, No, I don't have the balls for that. And then he said, You should think about it. You're beautiful.

And I'm just in shock. Because no one's told me that my whole life. I'm under no illusions, but it sure felt good.

So we went our separate ways, with a plan to see each other later that night. But I couldn't leave my hotel room. I felt like I'd been hit by lightning. What was I doing? I was almost in shock. I don't know if it was him, or everything converging.

The next day, on my way to the airport, I sent him a text saying I really appreciated the encouragement. He said, Life is to be lived, and you have to have adventures.

We continued to text for about a week. And then it turned out we were both heading to the same city for business trips. He asked me to dinner.

I had been faithful to my husband for 27 years. But no more.

The next week we were both in the same city for business again. Same thing.

A month after I met him, I told my husband I wanted a divorce.

It wasn't because of this individual. It had nothing to do with that. Well, not nothing. But it was such a momentum thing — it was just amazing.

It was eye opening. There is a life out there for me. What I have gained from this person has been remarkable. It's just a tiny chapter in all of my life, but the impact has been massive.

And it just gave me so much confidence. It probably saved me a million dollars in therapy. I really think it did.

We still communicate, but he's legally married. My feeling is, I'm working hard to have a life where I can be open and honest with people, and I can't get past the fact he's still married. If it was up to him, we'd still be doing our thing. But I just don't feel that's right for me. I want to be with somebody where I can live in the open, say their name, take a picture together.

But I have no regrets.

My life, sexually speaking, was very vanilla. He is not vanilla. I was just happy everything worked for me. I was so relieved I couldn't stand myself. It had been ten years. I couldn't believe how detached I'd become from that part of my life. How I'd believed that it wasn't important. I had shut it out.

I moved swiftly. It just propelled me to tell my husband that I wanted a divorce. And it was not received well. He knows nothing about this other person, and he never will.

He was extremely resistant. Horrifically resistant. And has been. We did mediation. So it's been basically a low conflict divorce. I agreed to pretty much everything.

He's a narcissist. I realized I had to play to his ego. I would say things like, I know you'll find someone that you really love. And feel passion for.

I put in the divorce agreement that I wouldn't make any claim on his earnings from his career, because he still thinks he's going to be globally famous. He says that when he wins an award, he's going to stand up and say, This is for my ex-wife who didn't believe in me. And I said, You get to say anything you want.

I feel so happy, and so hopeful. I had not felt hopeful about the future in soooo long…

It feels uncertain, really uncertain. But before when I would think about the future, it had a hopefulness about it. I haven't been through any loneliness yet, and that may be a problem at some point.

I'm currently doing some online dating, and it's not going well.

I have not been hearing back from men I'm interested in. But I do hear from a lot of toothless wonders — they're coming out of the woodwork. There's a lot of that. And it makes me uncomfortable. And then there were a couple times when I think I was communicating with someone who may not have been who he said he was.

So at this point, I'm not really ready to do a lot of dating. I just don't feel comfortable telling the kids I'm going out. I don't want to worry about that.

All of my married friends have been extremely supportive. There has not been one person who's said, Did you do everything? Did you try everything? That's been another thing that's been so awesome for me, the support that I've gotten. It's amazed me.

I finally got on Facebook. I was shut off before. Close with people who knew me, but not putting it out there. For me, this has been a liberating, empowering, terrifying, fulfilling, anxiety producing, experience. I've been through more emotions the past year than I had in the previous twenty.

When I tell people I'm divorced, a lot of them say, I'm sorry. But I say, Oh no, give me a fist bump. I am so happy.

And then there are other people who say, Oh my God, I'm so jealous that you're divorced.

You know, we did many things wrong. We didn't spend time together as a couple. But I don't think it would have changed the outcome.

A lot of women don't have economic independence. So that makes it precarious for them. And then there are the men who are afraid of giving up half of what they've got.

If someone had ever told me I would have stayed married for my kids, I never would have believed them. But then it happened. I wanted to get divorced ten years before I did, but I couldn't wrap my brain around sharing my kids. And not seeing them.

My relationship with that other man was like a rounding error in my marriage. My ex would blame it, but it wasn't the cause.

I had begged my ex to work on his sexual issues. He never wanted to even talk about it. He would shut down. I found that I need a stronger, more confident guy. I came to understand that I'm somewhat submissive. And he wasn't like that. We were completely opposite. He was never the type to say, Okay baby, it's going down…

But he never really had a high sex drive. Never. It was a bad match to begin with. He would be turned off to anything that wasn't vanilla.

And that turned me off — being rejected like that. I must be a big hussy, and he doesn't like it.

I tried to get him to go to the doctor, but he never would. He'd say, I'm fine, I'm fine, don't worry about it. There was nothing, no physical affection at all. No hand holding, no ass grabbing. Nothing.

My illicit lover – I don't really know what to call him – he was very sexual, and very experienced. Surprisingly so. Just in the time with him, with someone who adored every inch of me, was complimentary about every inch, it propped me up, it just gave me so much confidence. It was crazy.

And he'd tell me, you're going to have to date younger. There's no way an older guy is going to be able to keep up with you. But I want men who are age-appropriate.

I feel so much better now about myself, and my body.

He's the only guy I've been with so far, and I worry that he might have ruined me. My friends keep telling me I'm going to find someone who will give me all that, and also love me, and want to commit to me. Intellectually, I believe them. But emotionally I'm not there.

It's a blessing, to be at this point in my life, and have a new beginning.

Tina: It Just Gets So Discouraging

Tina is in her mid-fifties. Six years ago her husband shockingly declared he needed his space and had rented an apartment. Not so shocking: he'd taken up with a younger woman. Tina has moved on, pushing through the experience of dating in her fifties. She found the online approach horrible, never meeting anyone worthy of a second date. She had a brief relationship end when the guy went back to his old girlfriend. She tried an older man, but he couldn't keep up with her. And she's frustrated by the supposed "third-date" rule that says the man will move on if the woman isn't ready for sex by date three. She's hoping to get it all figured out someday, feeling she's wasting some of the best years of her life.

My divorce was a big surprise.

We had relocated down to Florida, sort of moving to our retirement home ahead of time. We wouldn't have to battle the weather. And with the kids finishing up college, I was hoping they'd end up here, also.

After about a year of living here, my husband just came home one day and said he had an apartment, and needed his space. It was completely out of the blue. I had no clues. Nothing. After being married 26 years.

Of course, there was someone else. She's fifteen years younger, and was married, with young kids.

I went back and forth with him for a year. Moving in and moving out. I basically just said, We're not communicating well. I really think it would be good to see a counselor. I gave him three different names and numbers, and said, You just tell me where and when to be there, and I will. But he never called any of them.

He moved out a fourth time, and we were separated for a couple months. And then I finally asked for the divorce.

He said he was surprised. He thought I'd still just want to stay separated.

I said, No, I feel like I haven't been married for the past year anyway.

He married her as soon as the divorce was final. I'm not in touch with him or them or any of it. I know the kids are in contact with their dad. I want them to be. But I also told them at the onset that I don't want to hear what he has going on.

He was a good dad and a good husband for a long time. And I don't know if he just flipped out, or what happened. Basically, I don't really talk about him with the kids. And they don't really talk about him with me.

If there were issues he had with the marriage, if there was a lack in the marriage, I never had a clue. He never said anything. We were partners, we made the decision to come down here together. We were both excited. I don't get it. I don't know.

We were having sex four or five times a week. So it wasn't sex. I don't know what it was, I really don't.

I still don't really have a grip, six years past, on where the weakness was, or what the issue was. And I wonder sometimes if I could talk to him about it. Though I'm not sure I could even believe what would come out of his mouth at this point...

So I was all on my own down here. Where I don't know anybody.

I tried online dating, but it was horrible because, well, I'm not sure. I felt the need to be polite, and respond to messages. But some of them were just, Hey baby — they were just sending the same thing to fifty other women. And then other men would send you this small novel about their life.

If the man picks up something from your profile, and puts it in the correspondence, at least he actually read my profile. And he's not just sending the same thing to me and fifty other women. I actually kept a spreadsheet — there was one guy using two different identities, but it was the same person.

I met a few for coffee, but generally knew right away I wasn't interested. A lot of the guys would tell me why their marriage didn't work, or why their last relationship didn't work, and how horrible she was. And I'm thinking, I don't want to talk about this.

To me, the past is the past. If you want to get into it later, that's fine. But when you sit down for an initial conversation with someone, it should be like, Where are you at now? What are you into now? I didn't know what they were looking for — email pals, or arm chair shrinks, or what?

It just wasn't a great experience. There wasn't anybody I met who I really wished I could have had a second date with. And some of them were just plain wacky. And of course the yup with a baseball cap and every other tooth, who uses a picture of himself in the bathroom mirror, but I'm like, No....

My self-esteem at the time was really low. I was very sensitive, and afraid of rejection. The whole dating thing, after being married so long, just seemed so awkward. But I think I've gotten past that.

I'm in a Meet-up group with other women in their forties and fifties who are also divorced. So we get an opportunity to talk a little bit about our experiences. For a lot of the women doing online dating, the pickings are slim, to be honest with you. They really are. I haven't heard of any big success stories. And I'm in a decent sized city.

I did have a relationship with a man that lasted about a month. He'd just moved down here also. We got along so well that he decided to move back to Wisconsin to be with his old girlfriend. (laughs)

We actually became decent friends, and we continued to see each other socially a bit since he didn't leave right away. And I told him, I really appreciate you being honest with me, telling me about your girlfriend, and that you're not taking advantage of me. Because he could have kept sleeping with me the whole time, and then just not showed up at some point. So I appreciated that. I thought that was pretty admirable.

There was one guy, I thought, Okay, let's try an older guy. The guys my age are looking at younger women. So this guy introduced himself to me and asked if I had a boyfriend. And I said, No. We went out a few times. And had a bit of a relationship. But he's probably eight years older than me, and he just couldn't keep up. I'm sorry. He couldn't even walk around the block. And I thought, No, I'm sorry. So that didn't work out.

Having sex with someone new for the first time wasn't such a big deal. Sort of like, What the heck, here we go. I didn't have a lot invested. And you're not looking for a life partner at that point. I felt a little less inhibited. Because I felt, I really don't care. We'll throw this out there. And if it's good, it's good. And if it's not, it probably won't happen again.

I had met my husband at sixteen. So I didn't have a lot of sexual experience. I've had more sexual partners since I've been divorced than I did before marriage.

I've talked to other women about this topic. And one of them said that with society the way it is now, with women able to reach out and contact men they're interested in, it's great we can be more assertive. But then, when you're dating someone, generally, they hear that if there isn't sex by the third date, they're on to the next one. So how does a female maintain that relationship?

Personally, I can't do casual sex. I tried to have a fun-buddy with one of the relationships, but it just did not work out. He would have been more than happy, he'd still more than happy — and it's been years. All I'd have to do is say the word. But I can't do that. When I have sex with someone, it's because my relationship has gotten past the casual point. It's past that. I want us to be more committed. I want to be more involved.

So it can be hard to get a relationship past that third date if there's that rule. I do hear that this happens frequently. I think a lot of men feel like they have plenty of options, and if you're not ready by date three, they can just move on.

I find more often than not that divorced guys over fifty are looking for younger women. They figure, Hey, I hit the gym, I've been there, done that, I've got some disposable income, no responsibilities, got a boat, whatever, and that's what I'm gonna go after.

It's kind of discouraging.

People don't approach me, even when I'm out with my girlfriends. Very rarely do we get approached. Even just general conversation. Unless they're like seventy, and figure they've got nothing to lose.

For my ex-husband, to get involved with a woman who had children in middle school, that struck me as very strange. I'm thinking, Really? Ours are college aged. We're done. They're launching.

At first, selfishly, I didn't want to date a guy with kids around still. But now, I'm at the point where it might be nice to have every other weekend to myself when he's got his kids. So I've changed my stance on that.

I think about my ex-husband, with his wife fifteen years younger. That means when she's my age, he'll be seventy. I sure wouldn't want to be lying next to a seventy-year-old now.

I do everything. I volunteer for the city. I volunteer with Meet-up groups. I take classes. I take classes through church. I'm everywhere. I'm very involved and out there. And I don't know what the hesitation is from men. I don't know. Is it scary for them to come up and talk to a woman?

I have a friend who has a doctorate. She's blond, gorgeous. Very out there physically, very comfortable with her body. And she's got an amazing body. So she's a smart woman, and she's very friendly, but she says the same thing. One of the guys in the group talked to her, and said men find her intimidating. I said, Really?

So we're trying to figure it out before we're seventy.

The ice breaker thing for a woman, it's hard to know how much is too much, or what's not enough. Is it appropriate, or not appropriate? I guess you just have to play it as you go.

I've done a lot of reading, I've spent time on a lot of divorce sites. But after a while, there's only so much you can take.

Honestly, I feel like I'm wasting some of the best years of my life. Because I'm not sharing them with someone.

I've got time. There's a little bit of money. There's no kid factor to worry about. You can make plans and do things. And you've got a little more freedom. There's the maturity that comes with it. I really do feel, partner-wise, I'm wasting some of the best years of my life.

I check my face and hair before I walk out the door. I look presentable. I'm not a high-maintenance girly-girl. I can clean up well. And I can put siding on a house.

I'm not a bar person. What are the odds of meeting the kind of guy I want in a bar? Where's that guy who wants to put some steaks on the grill, open a nice bottle of wine, and we'll see what's playing on Netflix? Or go for a drive in the mountains tomorrow?

We don't have to worry about getting pregnant. And we don't have to get up in the morning with our kids. That stereotype of the man having to beg the reluctant woman for sex is so untrue. I don't know how to get that across.

It was my fiftieth birthday, my girlfriend and I sat down on my sofa, with a bottle of wine and our laptops, and did an online dating profile. She clicked on a guy by accident, sent him a wink. She didn't know what she was doing. And now they're married. She went out on one date with him, and they ended up getting married, and now she has some house on the water. It was my birthday!

And I got a date with that guy who went back to his old girlfriend in Wisconsin.

They talk about reinventing yourself after divorce. Well, quite honestly, I was really content where I was.

I guess I have to stop taking things so personally, and be a little bit light-hearted with it. And have a little bit of fun.

But it just gets so discouraging.

Roger: I Have Not Cried Once

Mid-fifties Roger was married for 26 years. Roger's wife was verbally abusive and volatile. She was extremely materialistic, constantly demanding more and better. She even insisted that if Roger went golfing, she was entitled to spend an equal amount on herself. The sex life was disappointing. Roger wanted out of his marriage for a decade, but endured all that because of their financial situation. Finally, when real estate prices rebounded, he moved forward with the divorce. Roger has done none of the grieving so many divorced men and women experience. He's happy living in his two-bedroom apartment, golfing on the weekends, thrilled to be out of the marriage.

I was in my first job out of college, living in an apartment. She moved into the same building. She was a single mother, with a daughter.

We dated for a few years, then got married. We had our son very soon after. Later we moved back to my hometown for my work.

Early on we had a fairly decent marriage. Good times, bad times. But she always had a verbal temper. Any thought that came to her mind came out. Whether it was rational, reasonable, or not. Her daughter and I typically bore the brunt of that. She never did it to our son. He witnessed it.

My wife hadn't come from a lot of money. She became very much about living to impress other people. Keep up with the Joneses. And there was a lot of that where we lived.

I always felt like I needed to provide a lot. It was like, These people have this house and this car. And they're taking these nice vacations. So I felt a lot of stress to provide. I was never saving as much as I wanted. We were always kind of living on the edge.

All through that time period, she'd always say something, or we'd get into an argument or fight, and I would tell her, I'm not going to talk to you until you apologize. A lot of the fights were on

Sundays — and it would be Wednesday before we would speak again.

There were times during our marriage when we'd get into arguments and she'd say, Do you want a divorce? We should just get a divorce.

Her treatment of me was up and down throughout the whole marriage. But I'm a fighter and I'll stick with something. My parents were married 64 years. Her parents were married over 60. We just came from families where you didn't get divorced.

When my son graduated high school in 2007, at the height of the real estate market, we built a bigger house. And she became totally into the house, and what it was like, and everything like that.

And in the back of my mind, because we never were able to save enough money because she had to keep up with the Joneses, I knew that if I left in the marriage, she'd probably have kept the house, but I'd end up in a one bedroom apartment. And so my living arrangements would have been terrible.

I can specifically remember one time I was thinking about a divorce, but I said, I can't. We built the house, and then we went underwater. I wasn't willing to take a hit on the house.

In a way, it was a subconscious decision: This is where I'm at. So let's just keep trying to make the best of it.

And then about three years ago, my older brother got a divorce. In his situation, he and his wife grew apart, and just didn't do a lot together. So he was the first one to get a divorce. And I saw how my parents treated him. They were disappointed, but accepted it. I thought, Man, my older brother kind of paved the way for me.

We took a vacation last year. She got furious at me about driving directions. I can remember sitting in the car, and I said to myself, You've got to get out of this relationship. You've got to get out.

It was vacation. She's supposed to be happy. I'm taking a week off of work. We're supposed to be having the time of our lives.

It was awful. We never had sex. And we never had sex the whole summer after.

Our sex life was never what I wanted. I can probably say that in twenty-five years of marriage, I can count on two hands the number of times she initiated it. Eighty to ninety percent of it was maintenance sex, as one of my therapists described it. She just felt that as a wife, she was supposed to do it. Ten to twenty percent of the time she was into it.

But there were so many times I tried to get something started, and she wouldn't want it. So I'd just say, Fine, I'm over it.

You get shot down so many times, you just give up. She really used it as a weapon. And it wasn't like she was withholding something so great. It wasn't that at all.

I could never get her to sit down and do a budget. All she'd ever do was say, If you go golfing, then I'm entitled to spend that same amount of money on me.

I'd say, how about the fact that your hair colors and stuff costs $175, and my haircuts cost $15? Well, that's not the same thing, she'd say. Do you want me to look pretty or not? Quite honestly, I didn't really give a shit. I don't really care if you've got big tits, 'cause if all I can do is look at 'em and never touch 'em, so what?

So there were those things. And I would think, So this is what marriage is like? This is what I have to look forward to the next ten years of my working like, and then retired life?

About a year ago I started to see a therapist. And I asked him, Is this really the way it's supposed to be? And he said, That's what you live with? And I said, Yeah. And he told me, No, that's not the way it's supposed to be.

So I came to my decision about divorcing last summer. But because of family commitments and the holidays, I waited until January of this year to do it.

I started really trying to hint to her. Really give her the idea that I was going to do this. I started sleeping in another bedroom around the holidays. She kept asking what was going on.

I had read up about what could happen when I told her. They said to hope for the best, prepare for the worst, in terms of her reaction.

One Friday night, it came down, and I told her, Yep, I want a divorce.

And she said, Okay, but you have to tell the kids. I said I would. But then she called both the kids to tell them before I could. She lied to my son and said I was having an affair with my assistant, which was absolutely not true. At all.

With our daughter, all she cared about was that I was doing okay. My relationship with her, who's not biological, has been incredible. She always called me Dad. We've always been really close. I talk to my daughter every day.

A week later, I moved out. I stayed in a motel for about a week.

I went to get all my stuff from the house, but she had changed the locks. So I had to keep going back because she wouldn't let me be there very long.

She accused me of stealing her wedding ring and pawning it and keeping the cash. I swore to her I absolutely did not. A week later, I asked if she ever found it. And she was like, Yeah. That was so typical of her: Never told me, never admitted she was wrong.

I just recently started going on a dating site. I've communicated online with some women. And wow, there really are a lot of women out there. Just about every one of them says she's easy-going, great to get along with... And I'm like, Ummm, what's the catch there? You've got no baggage? Really? Everybody's got baggage. No matter what it is.

One night, in one of her moods, my wife texted to say how disappointed my dad would be in me. So she had to basically sit down and think, What's the meanest thing I can say to him? Then she typed it out, and hit Send. Unbelievable.

My ex is not dating. She is so bitter right now. Any man she'd come across would know it, and say, I'm staying away from this one.

I will have to pay support for a while. I'm sure she'd rather stay miserable and alone so I'll have to keep paying her, than find someone new. She won't want sex, so I know that won't drive her.

My wife was all about granite counter tops and wood floors. She used to be embarrassed by the house we had before the one we built. It was a fine house. Two stories. Three bedrooms. Great neighborhood.

When we were building the new house, I used to say to her, Okay, you have to be happy now. We're not taking vacations because of this house. So you have to be happy.

But later I realized that isn't what makes somebody happy.

I'm in a nice two-bedroom apartment. I golf on the weekends. I come home, I don't have to do anything. I used to do a shitload of yard work.

What I realized is, I did a lot of things to get myself out of the house. And away from her. I didn't realize how much I did it. But now, I'm like, I can do what I want. Don't have to do yard work. Mow the lawn. I don't miss that at all.

It's so nice not living to impress other people. I can live for myself. I don't care what other people think. I'm not gonna host people. My apartment is a mess right now. I don't care.

Before going through this, I thought I would have these nights where I'd come home, and just be bawling for an hour or two. Because I'm a sensitive guy. Much more than my wife. I have not cried once. When it first happened, I was like, Fine.

One of the best things I did was keep my situation to myself. I only told two of my co-workers. That way, I didn't end up getting a lot of opinions from everyone.

I only talked to a few professionals to ask if I was thinking the right way.

I do think that if it's not really bad, and if your kids really can't sense stuff, there's something to be said for hanging out and getting the kids to a certain point.

I'm glad I got my kids through all that stuff. College. Weddings. Because when I'm finally done with all this, I won't have to deal with it anymore.

Assuming I do find someone at some point, I wouldn't want to expose her to my ex-wife, even it was five years from now. I think it would be terrible.

I'm ignoring the advice that says you're gonna feel bad or unhappy. I just don't.

Sandra: Let's Talk About Anything But

Mid-fifties Sandra was married for 25 years. She has three grown children. Sandra considered leaving her marriage for more than a decade, but he's the one who initiated the split. Not surprisingly, it turned out her ex was already involved with someone else. Sandra continues to be troubled about her children interacting with the other woman. She found that her family and friends' efforts to be helpful actually made her feel worse, so she learned to set boundaries with them. Her recovery has been slow and painful, but she's moving in the right direction.

My ex is European. I'm American, but was living and working there when we met. We got married, and continued to live in Europe for a decade.

About 16 years ago, things weren't great with his business. At the same time, I had an opportunity to come back to the U.S. with my business. So we decided to do that.

I'd say that's when things began to turn bad. There was a lot of pressure. He was under so much stress with his business, which was not doing well. He hated being in the U.S. He had kept his business in Europe, and would go back and forth a lot.

At the beginning, he would go over every couple of months. And I was also traveling a lot for my work. So he took on the house and child care when I was on the road.

We kind of switched on and off. And that was very damaging to our marriage. It was all about keeping all the plates in the air. Keeping the bills paid, raising the children. And I think that's when the disconnect really started.

I debated a lot about whether to stay in the marriage or get out. My dad was living a couple hours away from us. So I went to him and said, You know, I have this job with travel, and I have these kids. And so, if I decide to end it with my husband, will you help me?

And my dad said, No. You get back there. You get married forever. And you have to do whatever it takes.

And I think that's something I held with me a lot. For many years, it stopped me from doing what I needed to do.

I think my parents' marriage was a good one. But they were old school about it. They'd say, This is what you chose, and you make it work. And it did work for them.

For a long time, my husband and I just existed in the same space. There would be good times. There would be times when it was fine. And it all worked. We had these great kids. And this nice life.

I very much held on to that. To those times when things were good. To the idea that I had this family. I didn't have a great marriage. But I pretended I did.

It was a lot like a holding pattern. There was a distance between us. My husband had a hard time fitting in socially here. I had a great job, I was making lots of friends, and doing what I needed to do. He was working from home, he was isolated, and stuck, and probably getting very depressed. I think he was suffering from a lot of depression. And I wasn't very helpful.

I was the stable breadwinner. My income paid the bills. His business provided the extras, if anything was coming in.

He never expressed any of that stereotypical, old-fashioned male culture. But I think he felt it. He thought he should be the one who solves the problems. And he could never admit that he struggled with it.

The sex life was okay up until the last five years. By then I'd gotten very resentful. And he was totally closed off. He never smiled, he was always angry or depressed. But then he would just announce he wanted to have sex. And I would be like, Wait a minute, you can't even smile at me when I walk in the door? So, that wasn't good.

I used to say to him, If you want to have sex, maybe you should clean the house. And then maybe things will be better.

He would do household chores, on his own terms, and to his own standards. It was fine. He was a great dad. He was really good with the kids. And he was present.

When my youngest turned 18, my husband said, I'm not doing this anymore.

During all his trips back and forth, he had set up a life for himself back home. And, he doesn't admit this, but he met someone. I think she put pressure on him. I think he would have just continued with our family, except she finally got to the point of saying, Wait a minute.

That's just me speculating. But I think it was a long term thing. And she must've finally said, Are you in or are you out? He'd probably been using the excuse of, But my kids are still home. Then when they weren't...

So he moved back. He left last summer.

It's actually a blessing and a curse. In many ways, it's great. I don't have to deal with him very often. And if I do, it's emails. And I don't have to share the kids, really. They're here, near me. That is a blessing. We don't have to argue about those kind of things.

But at the same time, it's hurtful for the kids. And it's also hurtful to me. It's like, Wait a minute, you just leave me here, with the bills and kids? How nice it is that you get to just walk away.

The way he handled it with the kids was kind of a mess. He left without telling them. Just took off. From a distance he texted or called them. And said, Oh, by the way, I'm not coming back. Which was really not okay.

It was awful for them. My youngest had actually known about his other life. She had figured something out when she was there with him. He had told her, Don't tell Mommy. Because it would be really horrible for her. So if you care about Mommy, you don't say anything.

She carried that around for a year. When he finally left, she said, Okay, now I've got some things to say.

My oldest is still in contact with her dad. The other two stopped talking to him. Blocked his number. He really wanted to see the kids. He thought I was keeping them from him. So I ended up arranging for them to see him. The kids said they didn't want to see him, but they really had to. He's their dad.

They all know about him seeing another woman. To this day, though, he doesn't admit it. He's a total narcissist. He says, No, you misinterpreted. Maybe I wanted to do this, but I waited until we got divorced.

He doesn't want to make the new woman look bad to them. Because he's at the point now where he wants the kids to be part of his life. He has to find a way to reintroduce her.

When it all happened, people said to me, Men don't leave unless there's somebody else. They're too comfortable. They still want to have you washing the dishes. As bad as things get, they'd still rather live in your house.

I have a really hard time thinking about my kids having a relationship with this woman. And it's something I don't control. They're old enough to do what they want.

Every time my ex-husband is frustrated with all this, and how the kids are handling it, I say, This is the path you chose to walk down. You could have walked down a different path. There was an honorable way to handle it, and a dishonorable way. You chose dishonorable.

I have my moments. I have my good days and my bad days. I think the first few months were really awful. I drank a lot of wine. Which wasn't helpful. I've got that under control again. Which is good.

The hardest thing for me is, when it happened, everyone wanted to talk about it. But talking about it was exactly what I didn't want to do.

That was really hard for me. I finally had to tell my brothers and sisters and friends: You know, I just really, really don't want to talk about this now. That was difficult for my relationships with my siblings. Because they thought I should be talking about it.

So they were sending me all this advice, and the names of lawyers. I wasn't even ready at that point to think about the legal stuff. I just needed to be hurt for a few months.

It's a really painful experience.

I've been in counseling, I have a therapist that I see. That's been really, really helpful. My kids have seen him as well. That's kind of been the glue that's held us together in the last year or so.

In the last couple of months, I've found that, Oh, I'm not actually feeling so shitty today. There is some hope. It's a hard road to walk down.

People say, Oh well, just get over it already. They don't think I'm recovering as fast as I should be. They're like, This was a really shitty thing, you shouldn't be feeling so bad.

Or they'd say, Oh good, you're relieved of all this.

The therapist really helped me. I talked about that a lot. The therapist gave me a script of what to say, in order to set that boundary. To be able to say, I appreciate so much your concern, and I appreciate that you want to help me, but here's what's helpful for me right now: Let me be. If we talk on the phone, or see each other, could we talk about anything other than that?

As soon as I set that boundary, verbalizing it in a positive way, they were really, really respectful. And really helpful.

I did make an attempt at doing online dating. But it wasn't great. I wasn't ready. The experience made me realize I wasn't ready.

It was all just awkward. Too early. That day will come. Maybe. I hope.

It's not fair to anybody. The nice people that I met. I wasn't ready to be there.

But the world of dating is very different from the last time I was out there.

Gray Divorce Stories

Overall, I think I've learned a lot. I've learned the buttons not to push with my ex. And the communication — I'm learning how to do that a little bit better.

We'll always be parents together. For a long time, I wished he would just disappear. That's what I said to him when he asked, What is it you really want? I said, I wish that I would never, ever have to hear from you, ever again. But that's never going to happen. We are parents together.

He has now become the dad of vacations and presents. But the kids know that, too. They're not stupid.

When he feels bad about the things that happened, boxes start appearing from Amazon. Presents. And the only time they see him is if he sends them tickets and they go to see him, and then they go to the beach for a week.

But that's the way it is.

Up until now, they tell me they don't want to see his new girlfriend. They have said to him, If you want to see us, it's us. No her.

Again, I don't control that. And I'm sure there's going to come a point where he's going to say, I have a life here, and you have to join in my life. And share my life as it is.

It's still not easy every day, but as someone told me, You just have to hope that at some point you'll have a week with more good days than bad days. And I think I'm there now. So that's really good.

And eventually, hopefully, it's a week of all good days.

Carol: Women Need to Be Proactive

Sixtyish Carol knew early on that her marriage wasn't what she wanted. Fearing the effect a divorce would have on her children, she hung in until the youngest was almost out of the house. While waiting, however, she began preparing herself for what would come next. Her path of self-discovery included meditation, tai chi, and reading about sexuality. Finally single, she began to date, including using online services. Which led to a shocking discovery: men don't always tell the truth online! She also learned that women need to take the first step, and if the man doesn't respond, it's his loss. Best of all, she's come alive sexually, saying she's never in her life desired it more than she does right now.

I was going to college, and met somebody at the hospital I was working at. And it was just more of an intellectual, professional relationship. I felt like he was really good for me, but it turned out that while he didn't abuse me physically, emotional abuse was his thing.

It wasn't on purpose; he'd come from an emotionally abusive family. He didn't know any better. So I fell for it, not realizing what it was, and literally gave my power away over a number of years.

When I was forty, I had some kind of flu, and picked up this novel, Outlander, by Diana Gabaldon. And when I put it down, I said, WTF, what have I done with my life? I am missing something.

But it was twenty more years before I could actually do anything about it.

I lived in a relatively affluent area. And I would see the divorced moms living in little apartments, and their kids getting free meals at school. While other kids were getting dropped off in Mercedes and BMW's. I didn't want to put my kids into that situation. I did not know what my rights were, as someone who'd given up a paycheck to be a full-time mom.

I believed that a divorce would be harder on the kids. And either way, the kids will never totally forgive you for breaking up the family.

Sex wasn't that great throughout the marriage, and then, pardon the pun, it petered out. It was less and less, and then finally nothing. I guess I just never found him that physically attractive. It was really more of an emotional, intellectual bond.

Still, there were a lot of things we did well together. We could plan, we could create. But still, it wasn't what a marriage should be.

Knowing that, I started down a path of self-discovery, with mediation and tai chi, and whatnot. And I realized where I went wrong, but it was too late to change it.

Finally, toward the end, I kind of tricked him into marriage counseling, which I knew was just to get him into a position where I could say I wanted a divorce.

I knew that when my kids got out of high school and were off to college, I was going to end the marriage. Things didn't quite go according to plan — one of my kids was still living at home — but I had to come forward and say something.

I was reading a lot of blogs. I found a great one for sex tips. It was funny, and smart. There are breathing exercises. And ideas for ways to be intimate, and have fun with yourself, and your lover.

I didn't let myself go totally stagnant. Just because you're not riding that bike anymore, and haven't for a long time, I was still preparing for when I was going to get back on that bike again. I was reading all this during our separation, sort of setting myself up mentally before the divorce was final. And then I decided, Okay, I'm ready, I've done my work.

It took a few months, nothing was happening, so I went on some online dating sites. It was a real learning experience.

I had a friend who agreed to be my dating buddy. He was someone I could talk to. We could share our experiences. So I got started.

I quickly found out there are a lot of liar-liar-pants-on-fire guys online. Including men who are married, and just exploring the dating sites to see who's out there.

I had some bad experiences. There was one guy, I refused to leave the parking lot. I just stood next to my car and talked to him. And then I blocked him. He'd been charming online, but face to face, just awful. He had said he was a doctor, but having worked in nursing, I knew he wasn't. Being my age, and having raised teenagers, I knew what a lying face looks like.

There was another guy who showed up, I thought he must be the father of the man I was expecting. But no, it was him. I mean, Please, how about a photo that's no more than three to five years old?

But early on, I did meet a great guy, and if he called me now and wanted to get together, I'd say, Yes please! But he's about four hours away, and after a few exchanges he never called me back. I liked him a lot, and I think he liked me, but we realized it wouldn't work.

I found that you have to be proactive. Women need to take the first step. If you send a little message and they don't answer back, well, their loss. That's my attitude.

At times, it feels like a high school dance where the guys are all standing along the wall, but you want to dance, so how are you gonna get 'em to dance with you? You've got to go up to somebody.

It is a completely different world now, compared to when we were in our teens and twenties. If women have learned anything, it's to basically state your needs. State what you want. State what you don't want. Get that all out there, right up front. Just don't waste each other's time.

I'm in my sixties, though my doctor just told me I could pass for being in my forties. I give an age-range of 54 to mid-sixties for online dating. People do tend to lie about their age. Also about being taller, or skinnier. I don't color my hair, so it's silver, which the hairdressers tell me is the color all the young women want.

I aimed at a younger demographic, but not too young, because then it's "What the heck are you talking about?" I need somebody a bit younger. I always insist on meeting for coffee or tea. And that ended the possibilities with several men who wanted to meet for drinks and to hook up.

There are so many women and men in my age group who are finding others of the same age and discovering, Wow, we can have sex for forty-five minutes at a time, stop and take a break, and then go back to it. We can do this. Young ones don't get to do that. It's like in and out.

Things are very different now, and it's actually pretty nice. But it also depends on how much work each person has done.

And now, in my current relationship, I just came alive. I have never been as horny, or desiring sex as much as I am now. Not even as a teenager, or in my twenties. I don't ever remember it being so hot. Honestly.

I told this guy, it had been a long, dry spell. So he went slow and gentle. Of course, it helps to have someone who has done a lot of therapy himself. It was just a perfect reawakening. I had no idea that I had such a libido.

When a man gets excited seeing you get turned on, that's it. You've got it.

I would tell men, Believe me, everything in your life is so much better when your woman is happy.

When I was looking for a house a few years ago, I made a list of everything I wanted in it. And I ended up being able to buy a place that had about 85% of that list.

Then I wrote a list of what I wanted in my ideal guy. It got up to about three or four pages, after some cuts and revisions. But when I met this particular guy that I'm seeing, I wouldn't even look at the list, because I knew he was more than 90%.

Setting your intentions, writing them down, and then revisiting them, says to the universe, This is what I want. And you put that out there. And it works.

Ellen: Now It's About Me

Late fifties Ellen was raised in an abusive home, and was desperate to find stability in her life. She married her husband not out of love, but because he fathered her child. She was the breadwinner in the marriage, paying for the toys he wanted; he never once gave her a gift. When she was seriously injured, he offered no solace. Still, she would have stayed married but for his cheating. Deeply depressed as her thirty-five year marriage ended, Ellen even considered suicide. But she has bounced back, slowly but surely gaining confidence and comfort in her situation. And after decades of taking care of a husband and her children, Ellen is focusing on just one thing now: herself.

We met in college. We did group stuff for quite a while. I wasn't really interested in him, per se.

Basically, we went out a couple times. And then I got pregnant. Immediately. That was our junior year. I did not marry him that year. We did live together at the college.

I didn't love him when I married him. It was kind of what was expected of you — you should marry the guy who fathered your child. And he seemed like a decent guy. So I settled.

I came from a very, very abusive home. Both my parents were alcoholics. My dad was a very, very mean drunk. I didn't want to have to move back home. My husband seemed decent enough. He was funny. He wasn't great looking. I had told him, if he ever put his hands on me in anger, it's over. And he never did. I was just looking for stability and a way to get away from all that craziness at my house.

After my son was born, I could not have any more children. We got a chance to adopt a daughter. My husband didn't really want her. But I wanted her desperately. He told me, If you get that baby, you can't get a new refrigerator. I went with the baby.

Things were comfortable. I was a teacher, and eventually became a principal. He's had his own business over thirty years.

He never was the money earner. I was. I paid for all of his toys. He had a lot of toys at the end.

I probably would have stayed married to him, because I took my vows very seriously. We were very involved in our church. He was on the governing board.

Sex wasn't great, throughout the entire marriage. We did not have sex very often, and it wasn't great, to be honest. But I was comfortable.

I had an accident, became partially disabled, and had to have surgery. I retired a little early because I needed a full year of recovery.

That's really when things started going downhill. He was not happy because I was not bringing in the good money. He never took care of me for anything. It was always all about him.

After my injury, I could kind of tell things were going on. I'd call up and say, Let's go to lunch. But he was always too busy. I called him once to say I was upset about some medical tests. He goes, Oh, that's a bummer. I gotta get back to work. At that point, I knew he was having an affair.

I found out the girlfriend is 37, the same age as our son.

He was texting her one night. He's an idiot, no lock on this phone. I got his phone, went through all the texts from her. She's saying things like, I wish I was there to take care of you. I wish I could tuck you into bed, and kiss you good night. I can't wait until we can start our life together. That kinda shit.

I went in and just blasted him. He was dumbfounded. I made sure he didn't sleep all night. The next morning I told him to get out.

You know what, I don't share very well.

Afterward, I had women come up to me, and say he'd been trolling around for a long time. My doctor, a woman, told me had propositioned her. Our dentist's wife told me he sent her inappropriate texts. There was a girl at his work who was ready to quit because he was so inappropriate with her. He was even inappropriate with one of my former students. Her mother told me about it. It was devastating.

I moved forward on the divorce.

We're in a fifty/fifty, no fault divorce state. All I asked for was the house, my retirement, and my car. But because of the way stuff got valued, I owed him a whole bunch of money.

When we were splitting up our assets, he wanted everything. He'd say, That's mine, that's mine, that was a gift, that was a gift. I looked around at all the things I had given him, but there wasn't anything that he'd ever given me. I just realized that.

Best of all, I got all the bills to pay. Including paying his Visa, where he took his girlfriend out on dates, and bought her a Christmas present. I liked that the best.

The thing that's so awful is that he was standing up, being an elder at the church when he was doing all this stuff.

I think I knew. But I didn't want to know.

A friend told me she got through her divorce by considering her ex-husband dead. You can't call 'em, you can't text 'em. You can't say anything to 'em. They're dead. And they can't hurt you anymore. They can't apologize, which he's never done. So I call him the Dead Man.

That was such a revelation to me. It makes so much more sense to me to think of him as dead.

I was going to kill myself one night. I felt so betrayed. I really was not getting support from my kids. They didn't want to get involved. I had no one. I had just had it. I felt like no one cared for me. So I got my gun.

I drove out to the country. I didn't want to make a mess in the house. I had turned off my phone, but for some reason decided to check it. And there was a text from a friend from high school.

She texted about going to our class reunion, which was coming up. I decided I was gonna tell her goodbye. She's the only one who ever reached out to me. Turns out, she lived very close to where I was. So I went and saw her. And it was like I was meant to be with her. She basically stopped me from killing myself.

That's how deep the depression was. And my kids just kept saying, Snap out of it. You don't just snap out of something like that.

I felt like a 58 year old fat woman, who had nothing to offer anybody. They had taken, and taken, and taken from me. I'm better now. I went back to the doctor and got more meds.

I realized that I can do things by myself. I have fixed plumbing here at the house. He left the house in a mess. I've been tearing out carpeting.

I'm slowly getting his bad juju out of this house. I'm making it mine. Getting rid of furniture, changing things.

I had my first sleep-over a couple weeks ago. I went to that class reunion and hooked up with a former classmate. We had never dated in school. But we kinda hooked up. He lives quite a ways away.

He came for the weekend. And I'll tell you what, I had the best sex I've ever had in my life. It was really freeing. I'm comfortable with him. He was married a long time, too, so I'm not worried about STD's. I'm not worried about getting pregnant.

And he told me that he thought I was beautiful. And I haven't been told I'm beautiful in a long time.

I was such a good girl. I had very few sexual partners. It was really hard for me initially. But he opened up something in me that I never knew existed. It was so much fun. We explored. We had fun, it was so dang much fun.

My son happened to pop in the morning that my friend was here. And it was a little uncomfortable. At least we were dressed, we were having coffee. But the guy was very nice to my son, talked to him. But my son was really put off by all of this. He has this idea that we're still a family. And we can still do things together. And get along, and sing Kumbaya.

It's not going to be that way.

When the Dead Man left, he told me that I was fat and ugly and he couldn't stand to look at me. I realized, I'm a normal fifty year old woman. I've got a little belly from having a child. I'm in menopause, I have hot flashes. Those are some of the things.

But my entire life had been about taking care of everybody else. Not myself.

Now it's about me.

And I think in the sexual sense, what I came to realize was, right now it's not about you, it's about me. It was really freeing.

I went out and bought my first sex toy. Never, never, would I have done this. I was so dang embarrassed going in. And you know what, my doctor told me to go buy a sex toy. I realized, it's normal. There's nothing wrong with that.

There was a gift I'd given my husband for a special anniversary. I think he loved it more than me. And he really wanted it back. You know, it's amazing what Cutco scissors can cut.

He doesn't get it. The betrayal was devastating to me.

I signed up for the "Our Time" dating website to see how that would go. It was an absolute bust. There are weird people out there. I don't think internet dating is for me. I only did it for a short time. I went out with one guy. And it was creepy. I would much rather have a connection. A friend of a friend. Something like that, versus trying to do these other things.

The guys my age all want young girls. That's what I see. They don't want women my age.

This whole year has been a year of firsts for me. First Thanksgiving, first Christmas. Birthdays. Other holidays. Some of our traditional things. Our anniversary came, and I didn't even think about it.

Things are going to get better. I survived. Christmas sucked. It was horrid. I tried to make it like it always was, and realized, It's never going to be that way again. I told the kids, I'm not doing it. I'm done. Don't want to do that anymore. Invite me, I'll come and help. But it's not at my house. And I'm done.

I made a bucket list of things I want to do. Things that push me out of my comfort zone. When I die, I want my kids to say, Oh my god, can you believe what Mom did?

And one of the things I have on there is skydiving. Next summer, I'm going to skydive. I'm scared to death to do it. But I'm gonna do it. Nude hot springs. I'm gonna go. Talk about getting out of your comfort zone! Because I need to prove to myself that I can do these things.

But part of that is accepting, Hey, this is what I am. I am not twenty. I do not have a body of a twenty year old. I never will. I have scars. I need to accept that they're part of me. And part of that is becoming comfortable with me.

I will never marry again. Never. I don't think I'd have a man live with me. Because I need my space, too. I want to be able to have my fun, but I also want to be able to kick him out, too.

I don't want to fall into the trap again of me taking care of somebody. All their needs. Because I've decided it's all about me right now. I have a right to be selfish.

It's been hard, but I've started telling my kids no. I'm not gonna do it. You know, you're grown, figure it out.

How could I run an entire school, be powerful, make decisions, have all these employees underneath me, and then be such a doormat in my own marriage?

I have my down days. There are down days. But I'm having better and better days. My biggest fear was that I couldn't make it on my own. And I've realized that I was supporting him all the time. I can stand on my own.

I asked a lot of people who'd been divorced if they remembered feeling the way I was feeling. And they did. I realized that all these emotional things I was going through were normal.

I had felt so incapable of handling those things. But then you get through them, and you realize, I can do this.

Jill: It Did Not Work Out At The Gym

Jill is in her late fifties. Though her marriage wasn't great, she was blindsided to discover her husband was seeing another woman — who he'd met at the gym they both used. It always hurt Jill when their daughter would spend time with her father and the new girlfriend with whom he'd been unfaithful. Jill was also hurt by the loss of her in-laws; particularly painful was their social media posts that included photos of her ex and his girlfriend. She's begun dating again, but hasn't found the man of her dreams: one with erectile dysfunction.

I met my husband at the gym. We got married two years later. We were older, in our thirties. I had to wait for the right one. Everything was good.

We had my daughter two years later.

When my daughter turned one, my husband told me he was going to quit his job. He just wasn't happy. I kind of freaked out a little bit. We had just bought a house and had a child, all in the same year. So it was a lot. But we worked through it, everything was fine.

He started his own business. That took a lot out of our financial life. But we made it through.

But then he seemed really unhappy with that business. It was always feast or famine. I asked him what he really wanted to do.

That led to applying for, and getting, the job he really wanted. Which was great – I was so happy for him.

He worked a lot, which meant I was like a single mom with my daughter since she was about five. But I loved, loved, loved it.

Okay, I'll say it right now: the demise of our marriage was that I loved being a mother more than a wife.

One day we had a fight, and he said, You know, I don't feel like being married anymore.

I was shocked. I remember calling my favorite sister-in-law to talk. She thought he was probably just upset, and that he'd never do that. He was committed for life.

So we continued along. Our daughter went to private school, played sports, and got into college on scholarship.

Then, about three years before we split up, he got seriously ill. He recovered fully, one-hundred percent. No residual anything. But since then, things changed. He went through a life-changing experience.

After his illness, we weren't having sex anymore. It was more platonic. But we still said, Love you, love you. Every morning, every night.

I think he realized he wasn't happy. And now he said he really wanted out.

I basically said, I think you owe it our twenty-something-year marriage to see if it's worth trying to save. So we went to therapy, and the therapist said, You guys are at totally opposite ends of the spectrum.

I didn't totally accept that. I do admit we'd grown apart. It was sort of the textbook, empty nester thing. But he didn't even want to go to therapy. We had another appointment, but he bailed out. Said I could go alone.

A lot of my friends, they said he must have somebody else already.

I had asked him: Is there somebody else? Is that why you don't even want to try? He said, No, there's nobody else.

And then two months later I saw him making a reservation for the two of them to Mexico.

I mean, I was blindsided. I had no idea. I wish I had known. He had found somebody. And she was twenty years younger.

I was devastated. It was about three weeks until I told my daughter we were getting a divorce.

Those three weeks were the hardest of my life. I went to work, and cried. So my boss knew — I had to tell him.

I just came home every night and stayed in my room. I was afraid to tell any of my friends. What if they said something to their kid, who told my daughter?

Finally, I just told her, Honey, your dad and I really love you, but I think we're at a place in our lives where we've grown apart. She wanted us to keep working on it, but I told her that wasn't going to happen. She slammed the door. She cried all night.

I went into her room the next morning. I had to go to work, but I told her to call me. I'd answer any question that I could. Ask me anything, I'll be as honest as I can. And she looked at me, still crying, eyes puffed up, and said, You have no idea what it feels like to be blindsided. You guys never fought.

And I did say, You know, honey, you're not the only one. And that's all I said. I didn't use the word blindsided. I didn't tell her who it was. I left it at that.

We decided not to go through a tough divorce. We decided to mediate. We got everything finalized within a year.

I had told my daughter, It won't be long before your dad starts dating. So don't get freaked out. And she said, It better not be one of those skanks from the gym. But it was.

In our settlement, I refused to sign unless he agreed to quit the gym. I couldn't make her do it. But I did make him do it. For a year, though, I had to see them there.

The first two years, it was horrible. Just horrible. They were living together, two miles from me. I would not go out because I was afraid of running into them. I kind of hibernated. I lost 25 pounds. I wasn't who I was.

Financially, I was more stressed out than anything else. I was working part-time. I didn't know how I was going to live.

My daughter came to me on Mother's Day. And I said, So on Father's Day, you should be with your dad. And she told me, No,

Dad said he's going to be away that weekend. I guess I'm not Dad's priority anymore.

That broke my heart. I said all the right things. You know, your dad loves you… She said, You're just saying that to make me feel better.

For the last game of my daughter's college career, I was there, waiting, a nervous wreck because I thought he'd come with his girlfriend. He never showed up.

She asked me why he didn't come. I said, You have to ask him. We don't talk.

Then he lied to her, saying he'd made other plans way before. But he hadn't. He knew when the game was, and said he was going to show up. It was so obvious what her father did. But you just don't want to drag them into it.

My ex and that girlfriend broke up after two years. Oh, and by the way, she's in jail now. Okay? Karma is a bitch.

He has a new girlfriend. He's very happy. She seems nice enough; I met her once. I really don't want to get involved.

But it hurts that my daughter hangs out with my ex and his new girlfriend. She's a very wealthy woman, they have a nice big home. And I have a hard time with the fact my daughter would rather be there.

I was just angry all the time. And jealous. Of not seeing her. But I also realize she's not a possession.

So I finally confronted her: How come you never come home?

She said, Well Mom, it's depressing at the house. You should just move. I said, I don't want to move. I fixed it up to my liking, so why should I move?

It took a therapist to help me see that every time she was with them, I felt the betrayal. Because I never told her about what happened. I just told her that her dad and I had grown apart. I never said a word about his cheating.

The therapist said, What would really make it work for you is, if your daughter came home and said, You're right. You always said this has nothing to do with me. It's between you and dad. But what dad did, he was an asshole.

She never did say it. But the thing is, once I realized that, I stopped being jealous. I stopped feeling the betrayal.

I think in her heart she knows what happened. She's never going to bring it up to me. And I'm willing to take that for now.

As long as it's good for my daughter, I really don't care. But it took me three years to get to this point. To get over being jealous.

I won't jump up and click my heels and send a gift if they decide to get married. I mean, I'm happy that they're happy. But them being good to my daughter is all I care about.

I think I did my job. My daughter is doing great.

A lot of men and women my age are going through divorces, and they all have their own circumstances. But I think the females are okay with not dating right away. The guys always seem like they need somebody.

I don't want to be a nurse with a purse. I don't want to take care of anybody.

I have a couple of male friends that I do a lot of things with. Strictly platonic. One's a widower, one's divorced. We text every day.

I finally said to one of them, and I hate saying this, I want to date a guy who has erectile dysfunction. I want a guy with E.D.

And my friend said, Why?

And I said, Because that's all they think about. And I want someone who likes me for me. And then if we need to rectify that problem later, that would be fine.

I did tell one of my gay friends about wanting a guy with E.D. And he said, You just haven't found the right dick yet. And maybe that's it.

I would love to meet someone who's divorced. They've been through what I've been through. I met a guy who's never been married. And I mentioned doing something with my daughter. And he was like, What? He just didn't get it.

I have a lot of friends who are still married. Unhappily married. And they all want to know what I'm going through.

They ask, What's the worst part? And I say, For me it was losing friends and my in-laws.

My hardest thing, and I'm heartbroken, more so than the marriage, is I miss my in-laws. We were always so close. We're still friends on Facebook. One of his sisters posted a picture, and wrote about going to the beach with her brother and his new girlfriend. Doesn't she know that we're still Facebook friends? And then another sister wrote about visiting, and going wine-tasting with them.

I know, life goes on. And it doesn't bother me to see a picture of him and the girlfriend. But it bothers me to see the sister-in-law and her husband with them. I was so close with them. I was in tears. I miss them. But I know they wouldn't hurt me intentionally.

I used to talk to them every other day. Now we haven't talked in a year and a half.

But I'm in a much better place now. It took me about three years to feel like I'm on top of the world again.

About a month or two ago, I was driving to meet some friends at the beach. And I said, You know, I've experienced love. I've experienced divorce. I've experienced betrayal. Everything. Child-birth. And right now, I just feel like I'm on top of the world.

I came out of it okay. I would have never said that a year ago.

I really do feel like there's a plan for me. And I just haven't found the right person yet.

I've finally gotten to a point where I'm financially stable. I can enjoy life. I have hope.

When my husband moved out, I gave him a hug. And I said, One of these days, I will thank you. I did say that to him.

Right now, I'm still not quite there yet. Not ready to thank him. But I'm glad to be where I am.

Things happen for a reason.

Rick: For Love or Money

Mid-fifties Rick was married just over 20 years. His marriage was difficult; Rick's wife was an alcoholic, a compulsive spender, and she refused to join him when he relocated for his dream job. Still, he loved her and was determined to stay married. That resolve crumbled, however, on discovering she was being unfaithful. After the divorce, Rick endured five years of misery. He strove to accept the fact of his split, yet found it tremendously painful to realize the life he'd dreamed of would never come to pass. He recognized that his focus on financial success not only damaged his marriage, it also slowed his divorce recovery. And he discovered that playing the role of victim was affecting his subsequent relationships.

I was accepted into two PhD programs, one very near where I grew up, the other someplace completely different. I chose the very different place.

And that's where I met my wife. I thought she was the most beautiful woman in the world. She was younger than me. And she was everything that I had not experienced where I grew up.

We fell in love, and then she got pregnant. I didn't want to get married, but my parents made me. But I did love her. We had a child six months after we got married. We went on to have three more. Things were great. I thought I was living the American dream.

Then we began to run into problems. My ex-wife had a very serious compulsive spending problem. Which she hid from me. That never stopped. It just got worse and worse over the years. The more money I made, the more she spent.

And it just led to so many financial issues. We always overcame them, by me paying the credit cards. But I grew such anger, and bitterness, and resentment.

I started distancing myself from her. I was not as respectful toward her as I should have been. But I did love her.

And I loved our family. We had a wonderful home, a big home. And I had a thriving practice. We were doing well, but we could never save money the way I wanted to. I worked really hard. I got up at 6:00 in the morning, and I didn't get home until about 7:00 every night.

We grew apart, and that's when her alcoholism really took place. The last ten years of our marriage she became a severe alcoholic, to the point where she got a DUI. With my daughter in the car. But I still loved her. I was not going to leave her over that.

At about this time, we all went to visit my brother and his family. I woke up one day and I said, I'm working like an animal, I'm making less money, and I'm missing out on my life.

I decided I'd try to find a job where I could really take advantage of all my degrees. So I started looking, and eventually I got an offer for my dream job. It was everything I'd wanted, combining my passion with my academic work. It was perfect. I had reached my career goal. But I'd have to move. And my wife refused to move with me.

So I did move — leaving my very nice, large home, to move to a one-bedroom apartment for that job. I was alone – no wife and no kids.

And then I found out, through my children, that my wife was being unfaithful.

I had to pray on it. I had never strayed in my marriage. And I just knew I could never get past that. And then I found out she'd stopped paying our mortgage. And she wasn't paying our second mortgage. I was sending my entire paycheck home. But she wasn't paying her car payment. All these bills.

All of a sudden, overnight, not only did I find out she was unfaithful, I also found out that she'd put us in such financial arrears that our house was now in foreclosure. She had also been siphoning off our retirement accounts. Which had tax implications. And so I was just devastated.

It was the beginning of an absolutely miserable next five years of my life.

The combination of infidelity, and then the money, were just too much to overcome. I could not even imagine how we'd recover. I knew she'd never stop. The financial piece had affected my retirement by ten years.

It was overwhelming. I had to make a very difficult decision because I chose to file for divorce while I still loved my wife. And I had nobody else. That's unusual — most people file for divorce when they have somebody else.

So I was alone. And living in a one-bedroom apartment in a foreign state where I had no friends and no family. I felt betrayed. It was more than I could imagine. I don't know how I got through it.

Later, I found out my ex used to leave our then twelve-year-old home alone when she went out, she was intoxicated almost every day. She was bringing men to the house. It was so bad, a judge allowed me to take my child out of state, and I've raised him alone ever since.

My oldest moved in with me, too, as did another of my children. The fourth lives away, but we're very close. So for all intents and purposes, I've got all my kids with me.

The divorce was bitter and acrimonious. On top of everything, I still had to pay her alimony for five years. I was really struggling financially, taking care of all the kids, plus paying her.

It was a tortuous experience. I felt this odyssey would never end. Somehow we got through it. My ex and I are now civil.

I was in a long-term relationship for about four years, on and off, and that was difficult as well. I don't think I'd ever fully recovered from the marriage, and I've realized I never came to grips with my divorce. I want to get remarried someday, but I don't want to be divorced again. I know I've got to stop picking the same kind of woman.

We had built such a great life together. Our kids were successful. We ate dinner together seven nights a week. And it was sad. My bitterness, my anger, my hostility toward her for her spending problem, a drinking problem, just made us more and more distant. And we ended up hurting each other.

I'm so afraid to make a mistake again.

My ex has actually wanted to reconcile with me. Begged me. Begged me to take her back. And for a minute, I thought about it. But we never got back together, never had any sort of sexual relationship.

But I was so lonely, and miffed, and I thought about that fantasy of what we'd had. But I knew I couldn't go back. It would ruin me. Financially and emotionally.

My head tells me I should get out of my current relationship, but my heart says to stay in it. I do love her, but I just don't have the faith and trust in her. That voice tells me that. But I don't have any financial ties to her. We love each other, but I think we both come with so much baggage.

I have actually been in much healthier relationships with other women, but then I pushed them away. Women who would have been good for me, and I just didn't feel attracted enough to them, and pushed them away. I ended the relationship.

That's so discouraging to me. And I am in therapy. Trying to figure it out. Hoping that I do figure it out.

It's not all gloom and doom. Professionally, and with my children, I have a great life. But I'm lonely. For friendships.

I think I've chased the dream of financial success, and I have it, but I've gotten away from the true essence of what a relationship is, and I'm paying the price.

I don't blame anybody for that at this point. I have to come to grips with it. My life didn't work out the way I thought it would.

I look at my friends who have remarried, who are happily remarried, and I'm not. So I feel like a freak. I feel lonely. I feel disenfranchised. Like I am not worthy of having a happy relationship.

I've been with women who treat me great, but they're not for me. I guess I haven't been through enough pain. I'm not used to being treated well.

I don't want to be putting down my ex-wife. We had a conversation about two months ago, and she said, I screwed up. And it hurt me. It was painful.

You strive to get to acceptance, but in order to get there, you have to accept a reality different than what you imagined in your fantasy. And that's devastating. Because that means that once you accept something, the life that you thought you had, will never be again.

That's just crushing. Because I thought we had just a great life. Beautiful home, beautiful area, both drove nice cars, blah, blah, blah. Everybody wanted to be at our house.

And I realized, if I hadn't left that to take my dream job, I never would have gotten divorced.

But I was so broken, so emotionally exhausted, from giving so much to my marriage, and getting so little back, that I had to leave.

I had to take a month off of work, I was so crushed by getting divorced. And so lonely. I remember driving this winding, rural road one morning, and I was so depressed, and I was coming around a corner, and I saw this big oak tree, and I said to myself, I wonder what it would be like to take my hand off the wheel and just end it.

And it made me realize I couldn't continue to wallow in my misery.

So here I am, five years later, recovering. And everybody tells me what a great guy I am. And I am a great guy. But I want true love again. And I don't have that.

I am starting to get out a little bit. Joined some sports leagues. I am trying to get out there more socially. And I am in therapy. Financially I am whole again.

I feel like I put money ahead of my marriage. What made me successful, and the goals I set, contributed to my divorce. I made money the priority. And as a result I ended up getting divorced.

And then, after the divorce, I made being financially stable my priority. Which really slowed my recovery from the divorce, because I was so focused on financial matters. I've come to find that out.

So as a result of all that, I didn't feel like I had anything to offer a new woman. Except financial disarray. And I had to work through that.

Did I hurt myself, and keep myself from having a loving, fulfilling relationship the last five years? Definitely. I felt like a man's worth is his financial standing. What can you offer a woman if you don't have anything?

But on the other hand, I had a son to raise. And I wanted to have the nice things that I thought I deserved. I had put the cart before the horse. So many people never financially recover from a divorce. And that scared me.

I realize now for five years I was running from the grief and the pain and the heartache of losing a woman that I loved. I loved her so, so much. I did not want to divorce her. It broke my heart. And I think I ran from it and used the money and the custody as an excuse.

And when I paid everything off, and felt I was back on my feet, and should have felt so great, I realized, Oh my god, I'm devastated.

I really do wish the best for my ex-wife. I will always be there to help her. She's the mother of my children. But it's just sad. The death of a marriage is by far the worst. Even more than losing my parents, who I loved dearly. Because that's your dream. That's your life. And all those dreams are dead.

But, it is what it is.

Getting through a divorce is not a straight line. It's peaks and valleys, it's convoluted. It's multi-layered.

I don't know if you ever fully get over it. You can move on. But when you start a marriage, if it means a lot to you, which it did to me, you're saying this is for life.

I want to get remarried. I loved it. But you know, it happened. And I'm learning from it.

I used to blame her. Now I realize I alienated her. I put money over her. It doesn't give her reason to do what she did, but I played a role in it, too. I've realized it takes two to get divorced. Not one.

For a long time I viewed myself as a victim. People would say, Oh my god, you're a single father, you're doing such a great job, how could she do this to you?

You know what I realized? By continuing to play the victim role, you guarantee yourself you'll continue to feel like you're being taken advantage of. And you just set yourself up for bad relationships in the future. I choose not to be a victim anymore. Moving beyond the victim role is not easy. But there is hope.

I was so depressed for years. It isn't until now that I've realized I am better off.

The next step for me is to figure out how to find the woman who satisfies me, and that I don't push away.

Alicia: Finding Her Happy Ending

It's been a wild ride for Alicia, who's in her early fifties. Both she and her husband had career ups and downs; she persevered, he sunk into alcoholism. She finally divorced him when he totaled her car. After about a year of therapy, meditation, and exercise, she was ready to date again. In addition to meeting a number appealing men, Alicia began to explore the world of sexual fetishes. She found a welcoming community of "kinksters," spending about a year as an enthusiastic sexual explorer. She's resumed more traditional dating, and has encountered more heartache. But she's back to being her authentic self, living her life with uncompromising joy — which she says is only possible because of what she experienced along the way.

I married late at thirty, and had my baby very late, at forty. I suspect that that had a lot to do with why things happened the way they happened.

I met my husband at a party. We really hit it off, really clicked. We had lots of idiosyncrasies in common, we could talk about old films. We loved Turner Classic Movies. He was my Leonard Maltin. The man can't jumpstart a car, but he can tell you who was the head of Paramount Studios in 1949.

We had a traditional courtship, moved in together pretty quickly, and then got married.

I'm adaptable, but realized I'd have to keep serving him, and his needs. He became more and more socially anxious, refusing to see other people. But I went along willingly. I wasn't a victim, I was a volunteer.

Our child really saved the marriage. I know they say it doesn't, but in this case it did. I could put all of my love and energy into this baby that I had wanted for so long. And he enjoyed the process of being the doting daddy for a little while.

We had to move back east for his work. But he got a great job at something he really liked. So it made the last ten years better financially. And he enjoyed going in to work.

The real problems started, where it did for a lot of people, at the beginning of the recession in '08.

I was in real estate. It had been going great. I was making really good money. And then he got laid off just as I couldn't get clients. I had told him, and I meant it, that I was excited that he'd have the opportunity to write his screenplay or novel. And it would be my pleasure to support him while he did so.

Instead, he started to drink.

I didn't understand it, and then I went into denial about it. It became a huge problem.

I had about a year of anguish. I had to go out and get a regular job because real estate wasn't working. Our daughter was in middle school. I was at work, he was in his home office, passed out on the floor. And she'd have to step over him to get money from his wallet to buy food. Those are memories no one ever wants their child to have.

I was stuck. According to the law, I could not get him out of our house, except in handcuffs. And there was only one time when that became appropriate. He was mostly just a brooding bitter, alcoholic.

There were times when I was at lunch, at work, driving around, weeping uncontrollably. I'd talk to my friends in different parts of the country, asking them what to do.

They'd say, Your daughter is resilient, you can take her away. And I'd say, And then what? What are we going to do, sleep on somebody's couch? I can't do that to her.

Then, one day, I let him take my car to run errands. His had a dead battery, but he didn't know how to jump it, and I wasn't going to do it for him. He didn't come home for four hours. When he did, he was on foot.

The best thing that happened was when he said to me, You don't have to ask me anymore, I'm going. He had crashed my car. Totally destroyed it. Not a scratch on him.

It was the end of the beginning. And he'd be out of my life.

My daughter and I moved just a few miles away so she could stay in the neighborhood, and still be in her school. I was a bit shell-shocked, of course, because there had been so much going on. But I had my daughter to take care of. And I got a great new job. I really did feel as if I'd moved on from a lot of grief. And pain. And anger. Oh God, I was so angry.

I spent about a year just recovering. I got myself a therapist. I came in and told her a shorter version of this story and said, I need to work through a lot. And she said, Yes you do. Friday at 2 o'clock.

I took care of myself, and did it in the cliché textbook way. Meditation, working out, taking care of myself and my kid. And I got back into life.

I was in recovery mode. It was very positive. Eventually, I was able to say, Okay, I've got a house. I've got some bank. I've got a good job. My kid's okay. I felt like a little groundhog peeking out of my hole, and looking around.

So, even if I wasn't totally ready, I decided to jump back into dating. I remember exactly how I got started. I was online, looking at New York Magazine, which I love, and I noticed at the top it said "Dating Site." And I thought, Oh, I'll just look around.

I figured if I was going to meet somebody compatible, they'd probably be reading New York Magazine. But you had to pay to use the site with additional information on the candidates. I said, Fuck that.

I happened to glance at a picture of a guy, which said, I'm at OK Cupid. That was the first time I'd ever heard of it. Back then, it was not that popular. Most people didn't know what it was.

I went over there, and started looking around, and I was shocked. I could not believe how many funny, intelligent, Jewish men in New York were there. Shocking, right? Great looking, funny, talented men.

I created a profile for myself, and boom, I jumped in. As I tend to do with most things.

There was a fabulous speak-easy type of cocktail lounge right next door to my office. I used it as my dating spot to meet gentlemen after work. We'd have a $16 cocktail. It's New York, right?

I really, really enjoyed dating. I slimmed down, I started feeling really good about the way I looked. I started to feel like a woman again. It's a wonderful feeling.

I got a lot of responses from exactly the kind of people I was interested in. I wrote in a style of someone who was articulate and intelligent. I think the term "sapiosexual" was not even in use then, but I made it clear that's what I'm looking for. If you don't know, it means you are turned on by intelligence.

I started dating a little bit, and meeting some guys. Then I got a strange email from someone who introduced herself as Chrissy and said, I am a cross-dressing submissive, and I know I'm not what you're looking for. But I need to let you know how charming I found your profile. And how delightful I think you are. And if you have any interest in anything, why don't you go to this website and see my profile. And I was like, What?

So I typed in that site, and went down a rabbit hole (laughs heartily)…

That was the beginning of some very intriguing erotic adventures that I allowed myself to go on. I became an explorer, if you will, a sexual explorer. Because it was the combination of the perfect time for me in my life: my kid was on her own, she had her own social life so she didn't need me except to be home at night.

I was so intrigued by so much of what I was reading about. I created my own profile, and started looking around. I started exploring all sorts of dark corners of the internet.

I had assumed that a website about sexual fetishes would be creepy, and it would be kind of uninviting. But I found just the opposite. It was a lot of fun.

They are very welcoming. They're called "kinksters." And they will explore everything except pedophilia. There are a lot of attractive, and interesting, and intelligent, very bright people on it. Good writers, too.

There are places in the middle of Manhattan where, if you want to explore physically, you can meet someone. Or go on your own.

I went one time, made out with a Michael Duncan look-alike who was into garter belts, which I happened to be wearing. I watched some amazing sex go on. And then I watched the BDSM stuff. I didn't want to do it personally, but I loved watching people, and seeing the whole scene take place. I watched breast-play. I mean, there is stuff going on that is fascinating. As a student of people, psychology, sociology, and sexuality, I was really enjoying it. It was a turn on. So yeah, I had a tremendous amount of fun. Exploring every area that I wanted to.

My enthusiasm was very appealing. I was a newbie, but I was very enthusiastic.

So that was my year of sex-ploration. I was always safe, and had a great time. I sort of got it out of my system.

I haven't been on it, frankly, in about two years now.

Then I started dating a pot-smoking psychologist, who was a real asshole. The red flag was when he used the term "healthy narcissism" more than once.

But I jumped into that one. We fell into using "love" way too early. He broke my heart, just pulled it out of my chest and threw it on the ground. It was very, very painful. We broke up over text. That was my first and last text break up. Text is a terrible way to communicate; it's a great way to miscommunicate.

Because I had been emotionally all the way in, when he broke up with me it was, at the time, shattering. I remember a moment when I was on the train home, and I could not keep the tears inside my head. Crying as hard as I could. I remember thinking, I'm so lucky I'm on train, because nobody gives a shit right now. I quoted Woody Allen to myself, like I always do, from Hannah and Her Sisters: "The heart is very resilient little muscle." It hurt so bad, but I knew it would heal. And it did.

I picked myself up, dusted myself off, and jumped back in.

I had another boyfriend a little while ago, but I broke up with him because I realized he was an introvert, and I can't settle for somebody who won't talk with me. But we're still really good friends.

And last weekend I had a fantastic date with a new guy, two dates in a row, with more to come.

It wasn't easy, but the payoff is wonderful. I can say that the last four years have been so much better than almost any years, and certainly the last ten years, of the marriage.

Most importantly, I can be my authentic self. And that's the most important thing there is to me.

I had contorted, to the point where I was not myself in any way. Sort of like coming out of a box where I had to comport myself like a twelve-year-old Chinese acrobat. To just stretch my arms out and embrace the world, which is my natural personality.

And I will tell you this: being in my early fifties was the best possible thing for me. Not only was I experiencing everything with this foundation of knowing who I was, despite all of the contortions I used to do for my husband, but I had the ability to understand what I needed. What was best for me. How to behave. I could not have lived this wonderful life the way I've been living, with uncompromising joy, if I had been in my thirties. And you can quote me on that.

Today, at work, they call me the lady who's always smiling. That's me, that's my story, and I'm happy!

I wouldn't have this incredibly fulfilling life if I hadn't gone through what I've gone through. At various times, it was extremely painful.

But what I learned is, you have to make your own happy endings.

Suzie: Familiarity Breeds Contempt

Early fifties Suzie spent her twenties building a successful career. Deciding in her thirties that she wanted a family, she set out to find a husband. She chose a man who felt familiar; only later did she realize that was because he possessed the same narcissism she'd experienced in her own family. Alarm bells were ringing from the beginning, but Suzie hung in there. She came to believe that the constant battles and the continual negotiations were normal. Five years ago Suzie began to consider getting out, yet she still gave credence to his argument that she should just be happy he didn't drink, do drugs, or sleep around. Finally, she was pushed over the edge, beginning a nasty divorce process.

By the time I was 29 or so, I was very much a career woman. I was flying around the country, I didn't have a lot of time to date. I wasn't sure if I wanted to get married.

But then I saw my sisters having children. And I was like, You know, this may not be such a bad idea. So I decided that I would purposefully date for the sake of finding someone to start a family with.

Back then there was no such thing as internet dating. But I could literally spend thousands of dollars on dating services, specifically to look for a husband.

And that's how I found mine. He was working as a school teacher. I really liked those hours. I thought it'd be great to start a family with somebody who had his schedule.

So he fit my criteria. We hit it off. We hit if off very well.

The thing about him, without getting too deep, and I've been in therapy, is that he's very much a narcissist. I'm the youngest of three children, and I was raised with narcissism.

He seemed very familiar to me. And what I didn't know at the time was, that was very unhealthy.

We were together and it seemed really good, but then he would do things that were not very kind. Alarm bells were ringing, but this felt good, it seemed all right, so I'd forgive it early in the relationship. I thought relationships were work. It felt like a norm. I didn't understand at that time that if it's like that at the very beginning, you're going to have a problem.

So we got married. We had a child a year later. Instant family.

He took a year off to stay home with the baby. Which was great. It was exactly what I wanted. However, it was really hard. He wasn't very supportive about making me feel like everything was okay. He was more like, I take care of the baby all day, and now when you come home, I want you to take care of her. And I want my time.

So we were jockeying for position right away.

We went to counseling a few times.

The first was when he decided to start a side business, which required lots of expensive equipment. So that created some financial pressure. And he's not a good business person. He wasn't tracking the books, he wasn't tracking expenses. It was almost like he had an entitlement problem. That's when I first started to investigate and learned about his narcissism problem.

When the counselor tried to talk about those issues, he didn't want to hear it, gave him the middle finger, and walked out.

We had our second child when I was forty. It wasn't as easy as before, but it worked finally. I took three months off for maternity leave, even though I shouldn't have.

I hated it, because I'm not that kind of person. We struggled again. We went back to therapy again. Again he did not get along with the therapist. He refused to go back.

The third time we went for therapy was a twelve-week program that has to do with appreciation, communication, conscious loving, that kind of thing. I wanted to keep going with the next phase, but he was like, I did my twelve weeks, I'm out. So he quit.

The turning point was about five years ago, during a big family event. My father-in-law, who's a moron, I really can't stand him, acted horrendously. And he caused a big problem, that really made everyone uncomfortable the entire weekend.

So what does my moron husband do? He takes his father's side, and basically makes it worse. My husband sent the message that he would choose his parents over me and our family. He would not do the right thing.

To me, that was like, Forget it.

That was the first time, five years ago, when I thought, I can't live like this. I don't mind being second to my children. I understand that. My husband was always second to my children for me. But I won't let him disrespect us. To just do whatever his father, or his parents, say to do. It's just a sick relationship.

When he refused to apologize, I decided to go see a lawyer. But at that point, all I did was start keeping my money separate.

I take my marriage vows very seriously.

My husband would say all the time, I don't drink, I don't do drugs. I don't sleep around. You've got it made with me. I'm terrific.

And he'd been like this for so long. And I was kind of confused. I'd think, Do I have it good? Really? Why don't I know I have it good? Why am I so unhappy?

At that point, I stopped giving him what he needed. He wants constant praise. Oh, my god, you are so wonderful. He really thrives on that. It's like a baby eating baby food. And I stopped giving that to him. I just stopped. I just did not love him anymore. I had nothing left to give.

Finally, last year, my family held an intervention. They told me my husband had posted a profile on an online dating site. My brother-in-law's sister, who's a widow, had seen him on the site.

My family was like, You've given him so many chances. We're here for you. You have to get out. We're not taking no for an answer.

So that's when I did it. I filed first thing this year.

But we're not divorced yet.

He's actually doing well financially, between his side business and being at the top of the teacher salary spectrum. But he claims I owe him alimony. So we're contending that.

After I filed, he actually tried to hit me. He had never done that before. And he was being really mean to my kids. He called my eleven-year-old a pain in his ass. Nobody wanted to live with him. So I went to family court, and filed domestic abuse. And I agreed to drop the charges if he'd move out of the house. So he did.

My kids are doing great. First, they were really, really upset with me. They didn't understand why, after all these years, it had to be now. It was a bad marriage for a long time. And when I had him removed from the house, they were really upset with me.

But things are so much better without him. They're both doing very well. He sees the younger one on a regular basis. The older one sees him when she wants.

They're actually going away with him for a few days. I can't afford a vacation, but he's taking them to the beach. And that's fine. They have a good relationship with him. I think it's better now that he doesn't live at home.

I don't speak to him. I don't have anything to do with him. We only communicate to set up events for our younger daughter.

He's all over the place, desperately trying to find somebody at this point. I thought I would try dating, but I'm not ready. I don't know if I'll ever be ready. So I'm not doing anything about meeting someone new.

I don't know what it's like to be single in my fifties. The last time I was single, there was no internet. I wouldn't even know how to begin looking.

I want my kids to be whole. They are my number one priority. And of course my career is my other number one priority. Getting back on my own two feet, and getting my confidence back.

I'm shaken up a little bit by this whole thing. And I have to make sure that I stay focused.

My job now is a compromise. I could be doing more if I didn't have kids. It's not to my full potential.

My husband is being very uncooperative. Discovery came and went, and he didn't give us anything. Because he doesn't keep any records. He's ignoring all the deadlines. They are not honoring the deadlines.

I'm on my fourth retainer with my attorney. We're pushing twenty grand since the beginning of the year.

For so long, I was unhappy, and it became the norm. I find it hard to believe that anybody out there is truly happy in their marriage.

People I never would suspect have approached me. I have this friend, who seems to doing so well, from the outside. She and her husband literally look like they have everything and a bag of chips. She said to me, Oh my God, I just want a divorce. And I asked if she'd ever talked to her husband. She said if she ever said anything, he'd want to divorce her. I said, How can you just go along and never say anything?

I believe people can be happy individually. It's just when you start to do all that compromising. You negotiate. In my marriage, everything was a negotiation. I'd say, Mow the lawn and I'll have sex with you. I thought that was normal. But how can you be happy like that?

We always had a sex life. For me, at least I was getting something out of this relationship. I work really hard. I wanted to have sex because I needed an orgasm. I'd know when I was getting to be a bitch at work. When I'm overdue. We'd make an appointment, basically.

But if he didn't mow the lawn, I'd withhold. You think you're getting laid tonight? Not if that lawn's not mowed. Not tonight. But if you mow the lawn tomorrow, you're on.

I'm not innocent in this. I went into it with my eyes open. But what a crappy way to have a relationship.

Brenda: I Wish I Knew Then What I Know Now

Brenda is in her mid-fifties. Though she admits to marrying for the wrong reasons, it lasted 29 years. Brenda thought she could change her hot-tempered husband, but failed miserably. One of the best periods of her marriage was when they separated for three months. She thought about getting out all along the journey, but it was several years after her kids moved away before she began taking steps to make it happen. First came individual counseling, followed by getting a full-time job. And then, when her husband launched into another of his abusive outbursts, she was ready to declare the marriage over. Even after all that, Brenda feels badly for her ex, who still wants her back. Brenda has learned it takes a lot of strength and courage to get divorced, wishing she'd had those traits sooner, but proud to have developed them now.

When I met my husband, I was ready to get married, and he was ready to get married, so we got married.

It was more about wanting a husband than being deeply in love with this man. I got married for the wrong reasons.

We had good times, and we had hard times.

I come from a very loving, normal family. I had a mom and a dad, and a couple sisters. Mom stayed home. We went on vacations, had holidays.

His family had a lot of anger and hot-tempered people. In the beginning, I really liked his parents, until I got to know them better. His father, especially. He had a hot temper. He'd yell at my mother-in-law. And my husband carried a lot of these things, too.

To the outside, it all looked good. We were a nice looking couple, we had two kids, they played soccer, we were involved, we both had jobs.

But there were many times when I'd confide in my friends that I didn't think this marriage was for me. I got married for the wrong reasons. I don't feel like I loved him. I just felt so stuck.

That was my mindset. Not all the time. Only when he would lose his temper. Or show his anger.

When we got married, I thought, I'll fix it. After all, he's with me, and I don't do that, so I'll change him.

About twelve years into the marriage, he put his hands on me. Not too pleasant, but it happened. Around my neck. I gave him an ultimatum: Either you get help with your anger, or I'm out of this marriage. So he ended up going to a counselor, maybe three times.

Then life goes on. He was nice. We continued our marriage.

We did counseling one other time about the anger episodes. The outbursts. We separated after that, for about three months. This was fifteen years into our marriage. He moved in with his parents. And then he started begging to come back.

Honestly, it was like the three best months I ever had. It was just peaceful, I could have my kids without fighting. Then he came back, all was well, the honeymoon phase again.

During the marriage, there were times when I felt like we were connected. And I thought, Wow, maybe we do have something special here.

Very rarely did I tell him I loved him. We just didn't say it to each other. I felt like as soon as the love started to grow, another episode of anger would happen. And then it'd be okay, and the love would start to grow again. And I'd think, Maybe this is okay. But then another episode would happen.

I kept doing things to change him, and mold him into the person I wanted him to be. But the bottom line is, he was never that person.

I love to read. And learn. And grow. But my husband isn't that way. He would have stayed in the same house until we were dead. He said that. He doesn't care. He's very content with very little, which is great. But I'm not. I like to see new things, do new things. Meet new people. And he's just not like that.

It's not right or wrong, but it is a big difference.

My husband had a very high sex drive. And I had a medium sex drive. He would be happy getting together five nights a week. But I can't do that. So we settled on one day a week, basically.

And that's the way it went throughout our marriage. He would get very irritable if it was longer than that. It was so important to him. And honestly, I didn't feel it was that important to me. Maybe that's men and women; I'm not really sure.

It was good to know we had the connection, but once a week was almost too much for me. Once a month would have been fine. If it was one day past once a week, he would get so frustrated if I said no. It would not be nice. No, not be fun. So, I kind of gave in a lot, almost always went along with it.

When I reached 53 or 54, I thought: My longevity is good. Do I want to live the second half of my life like the first half of my life? The answer was, No.

I struggled with that for a while. Three or four years.

A year ago, I wanted to move closer to our daughter. He was adamant that he wasn't moving. I thought, Okay, this'll be the end of our marriage. But, he changed his mind and decided to go.

So I was like, Okay, fine, let's go. Maybe we can keep the marriage going.

We moved, but one thing led to another, and we ended up moving back to where we'd been originally. And when we got back, I had this feeling: this isn't what I want. I don't want to be with this man. And that's when I kinda fell apart.

I felt really trapped. I went into a really dark time. Like, I don't know what to do. I cannot live my life like this. I'm living a lie. I don't love this man. I don't want to be married to him. But how do I get out of this?

So I went to a counselor. And she told me, You have to really listen to yourself. Listen to your heart. And do what you feel is right.

I knew that I had to end my marriage. I just knew it.

I'd been working about twenty-five hours a week for the last fifteen years. That was after staying home for seven or eight years with my kids.

Earlier this year, I got a full-time job. I didn't tell my husband the reason why. But I knew I needed to do it in order to take the next step.

I suppose some people get divorced overnight, but I think it's a step-by-step process. You have to be ready. And then you have to take the steps you need to get there.

Then my husband had another "episode." He screamed at me, called me a bitch.

And I said, That's it. I am never going to go through this again. He'll never do this to me again. Our marriage is not going to be any longer. We started sleeping apart. We lived together for a month after because of finances.

It was almost like it wasn't happening to me. It was surreal. So much to take in.

In my brain, I knew it was right. But my heart, it would break. Because when I saw my husband, he was a mess. There was a lot of guilt. When we first decided, for real, it was pitiful. I wanted to cry, but I tried to be strong.

He would come home from work, and say, Please, just love me. Just love me for who I am. Pleading with me.

My feelings were sadness for what I was doing to him. That I'm ruining this other person's life.

And it wasn't about my kids. My kids were okay. I talked to them, and they were both okay. It's not what we expected to happen. They didn't expect us to get divorced. But they're dealing with it fine.

After a month, I moved in with my mom.

I used to think, If he cheated on me it would have been easier. There's a lot of cheating going on. And that's such a solid reason to leave. I don't explain to people why we got divorced because it's nobody else's business. Except my close friends.

As the divorce was happening, he'd get in my face and say, You're giving up. You're giving up. And I was like, I don't think I'm giving up. I tried for 28 years. I'm not giving up.

I'm a go-getter. I don't quit. Okay, I did quit after 28 years, but I don't feel like I'm a quitter.

This marriage, as it was, wasn't fair to me, and it wasn't fair to him. He's not a bad person.

He keeps texting me. He says I'm the best thing that ever happened to him. He would take me back in a minute. But that's not what I want.

The divorce was final just a couple months ago.

It's hard to erase everything that's happened. I almost feel like I've been scarred.

There were things I wish I knew then what I know now. I wish I had felt the confidence then that I have now. But I didn't. I wasn't working. I was home with my kids. And just not in a situation to be on my own.

Nobody can tell you when it's the right time to get divorced. It's just something that you have to feel in your heart.

I have a very supportive family. They've spent a lot of time with me. And I've leaned on them. That's kind of held me up. And it's been my strength right now. If I was all alone, I don't think I could do it.

Through the years, I used to talk to my mom and sisters occasionally, and say, I don't know what to do. I don't know if I should stay married to him.

I'd show up in tears, because I didn't feel good about my marriage.

I didn't really tell my mom all the things that happened in my marriage. I just didn't want her to feel bad. But then she'd say things like, He's a hard worker, and I know your marriage isn't perfect, but he's home every night. He doesn't cheat on you. And so my family would say all these positive things, and almost talk me out of it. That's why I think I stayed, too.

I kept saying, Yeah, you're right. I tried to look at the good. But I think I knew in my heart what I had to do.

It had to be my time. I don't think I could have done it when the kids lived at home. And we would have had to swap them, This weekend is yours, this weekend is mine.

Things between my husband and my kids are better now than they were when we were all together. They've gotten a lot closer.

That's really hard for me. I keep my mouth shut, but I almost feel resentment. Not anger. I'm not mad. It's great for my kids. But I wasn't the one who messed up. I'm not the one from the dysfunctional family. So how come Dad's getting all the love now?

I almost wish they'd be mean to him, after all the years he was mean to them. But that's not what they want to do. And that's not healthy, I know.

My daughter said he needs the support now. I've got my family. His isn't that tight. I'd like to think it's the good upbringing they got that makes them want to be there for their dad.

Don't get me wrong — they're showing me love, too. I love my kids to death.

I have one very good friend who knew everything all the way along. For the past 28 years we've talked every week. For a while, when I first got divorced, I felt like she really drifted away from me. For six or seven months, she wasn't there. I didn't know if she was feeling resentful that I got divorced. We no longer chat about the problems in our marriages because I'm not married anymore. That used to be the connection we shared. She might be envious that I got out.

I sometimes feel that I'm contagious — things have changed with some of my other friends. Some have stuck by me, and some haven't. It's weird.

I went out to lunch with a couple of my girlfriends. As I was sharing that I'm getting divorced, they said they'd been considering it, too. But the fact is, a lot of people aren't brave enough to get divorced. It takes a lot of courage. And a lot of strength. You can't be a wimpy little woman. Or man. You have to have some strength about you, and a support system.

I'd be willing to share with my friends. I think I've learned a lot through this experience.

It's much easier just to settle. Honestly. So much easier. But I don't think I could have lived with myself if I didn't make a move.

I kept thinking, I don't want to be eighty or eighty-five and think, God I wish I'd gotten divorced back when I was fifty. You only live once. I didn't want regrets.

It's too early for me to start dating again. Definitely.

I'm not there yet. But I think about it. I would love to meet somebody in time, but not now. I really need to be a little bit more independent. I want to make sure I can stand on my own two feet. Pay my bills, I want to be confident in who I am. And I also want to be happy with myself. And where I'm at, before I put it on somebody else.

The next person I meet, I'm going to love who they are, not who I hope they can be. That's definitely something I've learned.

I've grown a lot. But I'm not who I want to be yet.

Fred: Not the Brady Bunch

Fred is in his mid-fifties. He and his wife were married to other people when they first met and fell in love. They divorced their original spouses, got married, and formed a new blended family. But unlike the classic TV show, there was no happy ending: Fred's second wife left him for another man. Fred has struggled; he's tried to focus on the child they had together, hoping to help him achieve the same success as the older kids from the previous marriages. As painful as the process has been, Fred believes it has forced him to examine his life, make some changes, and get back to being who he wants to be.

We met at work in the mid-90's. She was married at the time, I was married at the time. And we fell in love. I thought she was the perfect woman for me. And she felt the same way about me.

She got divorced first.

We had a rough go getting started. I was not divorced yet. I do not believe in divorce. I still don't believe in divorce. It's not the proper thing for the kids. I don't think it's the proper way to go, period. Having said that, of course, I'm now on my second divorce. I think you call that a bitter irony.

Eventually I did get divorced. It took about two years, and then we got married shortly thereafter.

So that was the start of the relationship. Going forward, we really worked hard to blend the two families. She had two kids, and I had two kids. That was our priority. That's always been our priority. The kids have always come first for us.

I thought our family would stay just the six of us: the four kids, my wife and me.

But then we had a child together. My wife wanted it more than I did. It caused a rift in our marriage. And I think that was the primary reason why we ended up being divorced, when the final analysis comes in.

Our son was born when I was forty. I felt that was late. I didn't want to be sixty when my kid was in college. Believe me, I love my son to death. But that changed our lifestyle and our expectations, put too much stress into our marriage. We tried to work it out by counseling.

During the marriage, our sex life started out fantastic. When we had our child, it became more reasonable. But in the later years it dropped off to nothing. Sex, and money, were the two biggest sources of arguments for us.

I had come to the point in my life where I was willing to compromise on things. I'm a touchy, feely guy. I'm gregarious. She's more buttoned down, very reticent.

And we went from having all that touch and feel to nothing. Roommates who occupy the same space. And I was willing to compromise and say, Okay, at least I'll get something.

For the last three to five years I had thought things were better. We were coming to a point where I thought we were going to be fine. Ride off into the sunset, as it were.

But then came the bombshell.

It was a weekend. Her cell phone went off. I pick it up, and see it's a text from a guy she works with. I've never met him, but I knew who he was.

I handed it to her, kiddingly saying, Hey, it's your work husband. He knows the rules — no texting on the weekend. I was making a joke. But she had this look on her face. It was just kind of odd.

A couple days later I get a text from her. She said, I don't really feel right about this. I don't feel good about this. I think we should get divorced.

We have this whole text conversation. She tells me she's met someone, and wants to explore life with him. She's given up too much of herself. I basically say, Okay, I don't want to throw away twenty years. I'll give you space to explore, and we'll see what happens.

At first she said that would work. But by the next day, she was already saying she didn't want to explore, she wanted it to be forever.

Which precipitates more arguments. What did I do wrong? What happened here? And of course it all tumbled out. That she grew close to this guy. They fell in love. And they've been having sex right along.

And I'm thinking, Let me get this straight: you and I haven't had anything to do with each other in years, and you're going to town with this guy? Like she used to go to town with me? When we first got together, because I was married, we weren't going to hotels. We were in cars. We were doing stuff like that. She's 53 years old and she's doing it in cars again?

I thought we had a marriage where we would tell each other everything that was going on. But obviously that wasn't exactly true.

It's been hell. My worst nightmare.

We actually still live together. I've been advised by counsel that if I leave I'll be hit with abandonment. It's incredibly awkward. And the source of a lot of friction, obviously.

We were actually sleeping in the same king-sized bed. Her on her side, me on mine. And then she said she wants her own space. I said, Okay, you left, you get the guest room.

She's actively dating, so I'm in the awkward position of having to be home with our son so she can go out with her boyfriend. It's difficult, and rather unique.

I don't feel a lot of jealousy there. The marriage is gone, and I understand that. I'm more concerned with the fact that I want to be very circumspect about who's replacing me, as it were.

Her boyfriend will eventually be living in this house. "Our home." And I'm not happy about that. We built this home together. We put our hearts and souls into it. But, on the other hand, my son doesn't want to leave it. I won't force a sale. I don't want to do that to my son. Just because Mom and Dad can't get along, that's not a reason he should have to leave his house.

At this point, I understand that my marriage is over. I get that. It makes sense to me. It doesn't make me happy, but I get it. And now the focus has to switch to our son, just like it did twenty years ago when we concentrated on the four older kids.

Whenever we've spoken to him, and we've done it together and separately, the story has been remarkably consistent. It affects his life and he understands it. Every one of his friends has a step-father, or there's an ex-wife. He is a product of a generation of divorced people. All his friends. His girlfriend. It's so commonplace for him. His only concern is we don't fight, and he doesn't have to move.

One of the primary good things that I always focus on is the fact that we were able to blend these four kids together, have one of our own, and all of them are happy, healthy, and successful. They're all doing well, and I attribute that to the hard work we put in together.

Today, that's all I can hold on to. Hopefully I'll get to a point where I can hold on to some other things. But not yet.

The group of friends that we had — almost universally they've all said this wasn't a surprise to them. They're happy for her, and that's how it goes.

There have been a couple of exceptions. A few of the guys have called me separately, and said, Hey, I'm on your side. I've got your back. But I always get the impression that they want to make sure I never say anything to their wives.

I've tried to connect with some of my old my friends from school. But at this stage, they've got their own lives, and their own personal issues. And it's tough to rebuild friendships that you haven't nurtured for so many years.

Of course, I didn't do that because I didn't need to. I had my wife. That's who I talked to. She was my sounding board. It's a mistake I won't make again. She did not make the same mistake. She kept close to a lot of her friends. Maybe it's a woman/guy thing.

I get the impression that people want to talk to me. People have been supportive. But sometimes I get the feeling they think

I'm contagious: You're divorced, and I could catch it. It's never been overt, but you kinda get that feeling.

I don't hold back as far as telling people what happened. They ask what's going on, I tell them my wife left me for another man. Maybe it's a way to play for sympathy, I don't know, but that's what I do.

I have a friend, who's been separated over a decade. And he's out there. When he heard what happened to me, he took me to this place that's apparently a stomping ground for divorced people. I was, I don't want to say appalled, but I'm going to say appalled. The people in this bar… a lot of them were fine looking people. But they all just smacked of desperation. I can't imagine this is how it is everywhere, but at this bar, at this time, at this place, people smacked of desperation. And I looked at my buddy, and I said, Is this what you do? And he said he goes to a place like this two or three times a week. And that scared the shit out of me. Wow, I am not up for this!

My first wife remarried also. Once we got past the initial "hate," we've always been cordial. She doesn't live far away. We actually built this house close to her, because she had custody of our kids early on.

She was one of the first people I told. And it wasn't because we'd been so close, sharing secrets, and talking. We were just two people who knew each other and got along. And had kids together.

And what I told her was, I'm sorry. Now I know what you went through. She was still in love with me, and I walked out on her. And since then we've gotten closer. She calls me out of the blue. Recently, I went out for a drink with her and her husband.

I've done counseling three times. When were first getting our relationship going, and my wife thought I was taking too long to get divorced. When we were having troubles after having our child together. And now, as I'm working through the divorce.

I really don't have a lot of faith in it. I think a lot of it is very self-serving. I think a lot of it is more designed to continue the process, keep you in therapy.

My wife would say she gave up her own happiness for the sake of the children, and for me. She was never really happy with me and our relationship. But she sucked it up, and did what she had to do for the sake of the children. And I can understand some of that. I don't necessarily believe all of it. Because you get a feeling for somebody. You have an idea after twenty years what it's all about.

But she said some things to me that really forced me to examine how I interact. And the things that I've done in my life. She said it several times: She never felt safe with me. Not physically safe: she meant she never felt comfortable, like "I had her back" safe.

I like to think that wasn't true, but I can't discount her feelings. Her feelings are her feelings. It's caused me to do a lot of self-examination. And spend a lot of time with a counselor who is hell-bent on flaying me alive and finding out exactly what my issues are.

She also says her current relationship is easy, whereas ours was hard. I can't discount that either. Ours was hard. We worked — at least, I worked.

It's difficult to realize that for twenty years your wife didn't think you had her back. I can't say it's necessarily wrong.

She claimed she brought it up in a lot of different ways, but it was never brought up in the sense of: Okay, here's the deal buddy.

I get it. She's fallen in love with somebody else. She wants a different life. But she never gave me the chance to fix the problems. And her response, of course, would be, Well, you can't fix that problem. But how could I know? I never got a chance.

That's my biggest regret about this whole thing.

I'm still in love with her. I'd take her back in a heartbeat. If she came back, having sowed her wild oats, that would be something we could work through together, and get to a better place.

The separation and divorce are a catalyst for me. For me to look back and say, Okay, what have you been doing for the past twenty years? What have you been doing for the past forty years? What kind of changes do you have to make in your personality to avoid this in the future? I'm not perfect. I'm never gonna be perfect. I've got my quirks. And foibles.

If I can take something away from this, and become a little bit better of a person, great. That would be the silver lining to this whole mess.

I had a plan. I knew where I was going to be. Retired by sixty, then off and traveling. It's not gonna happen now.

That bothers me.

But I am looking forward to exploring. Getting back to being the person I want to be. I know what made me happy in the past. Maybe it's time to start doing those things again.

Robin: Lean Into the Grief

Robin was married for 24 years; the last ten were not good. She had hoped that building their dream house together might save the marriage; instead, it highlighted everything wrong with it. She got into a relationship with a new man right after her divorce, and though it was fun, she knew it wasn't forever. When it ended, Robin decided to take time to both grieve the loss of her marriage, and figure out how to be alone. It was a dark, painful period, but she felt it was vital in order to enjoy better relationships in the future. She got back to dating, but has yet to find someone she wants to spend the next few decades with. Four years ago, she moved overseas, eventually starting a business offering tours of her new hometown.

When I got married, and I'm certain everyone would say this, I thought it was forever. I had no doubt that it would go the distance. I was raised in a very traditional family. My parents stayed married their entire lives. I never had a thought that I wouldn't be married forever.

My husband and I met in college. We dated some, but we each dated a lot of other people, too. Then we started to date exclusively while he was getting his MBA. After about nine months, he was offered a job in another city, a great job.

And he said, Well, are you going to come with me? I was teaching school. And I said, I can't go until the end of the school year, and I'm not going unless we get married. And he said, Well, okay.

Looking back, it makes me hurt. I think, Why didn't I wait for that man who said, Oh my God, I can't go anywhere without you? If you're not coming, I can't go. Instead, it was, more or less, a business transaction, mutually beneficial for both parties.

At the time, I just didn't really know what to look for.

So we got married just before I turned 25. He was 26. We both had graduated from college, he had an MBA. So we thought we'd crossed all the T's and dotted all the I's. And were doing everything right.

We discussed getting divorced at one point, ten years before we did. We definitely had a decade that wasn't good. I just wanted to get my children raised. I felt like that was a responsibility I had committed to. I wanted to do that.

After our last son graduated from high school, we found a piece of real estate in an area where we'd always talked about building a home.

We were very comfortable financially, though the relationship was fairly rocky at this point. But we thought this was the perfect thing. We'd build our dream home. It would be a project to pull us together. Kind of like you do when you first have children. We'd end up with this beautiful result, and it would bring us back together after some rough years.

But it was just the opposite. We agreed on nothing. He really didn't want to be involved. He just kept saying, If it comes in in the black, and not the red, I'm fine with it. Don't ask me.

To me, it just became a mirror of everything that was wrong. We weren't communicating well. We were living two separate lives. We obviously could build a gorgeous home and have all the comforts, but neither of us really wanted to be there with the other one.

It was really plain to see: If we can't be happy here, and if we can't work together on this, there's just nothing left for us.

Around this time, we did go on a trip together. As the forever optimist, I thought, Oh, this will be fabulous. We'll have this great experience. This will fix everything. We were flying First Class. We were staying in these gorgeous hotels. Maybe it'll put a little spark back in. He won't have his phone. He won't be working.

Our sex life had been nonexistent, but I thought it might come back to life on the trip, too. We did it just once, and I remember thinking, Oh, God, no. This is not going to fix anything. I just don't have feelings for this man anymore.

Shortly after we came home, I asked for the divorce. I just said, This isn't working.

He put up a fight about the finances, but he was done with me, and had been done with me, for quite a few years.

We did not have an amicable divorce. It really became contentious. Two things I learned in looking back at my divorce: First, people wait way too long to get counseling. I always thought if I brought it up, he'd say, Are you asking me for a divorce? Why are you doing this?

And number two, find a way to amicably split the finances. Or whatever the big hot issue is for you. Find a way to do it quickly. Or you'll make two lawyers very rich, and you will be very bitter.

I had been a really traditional full-time mom, homemaker. He was traveling all the time for work. Sometimes he'd be gone all week, home on Friday, then flying out again on Sunday.

I had worked part-time, but there was a big disparity in who had income. And the ability to make income. I didn't want to take him to the cleaners. I wanted five years of support so that I could go back to school and get on my feet. And he said no. Then the judge said, You can pay her for twenty-four years.

So that just led to all the ego battles. And that's the saddest part of our whole divorce. I would have been so amicable, and taken so much less, but he felt like he shouldn't have to pay me anything. Just divide the assets and be done with it.

We've gone our separate ways. There's not a lot of friendliness between us. But I don't feel any animosity.

He's just not a really warm and fuzzy person. So the kids see him every month, or every other month. Whereas, when I'm in town, I'll see them three times a week. It's just a personality difference. And for him that works fine.

He is getting married soon to the woman he's been with all of these years. Which started before we were divorced. She asked her husband for a divorce two weeks after I asked mine for a divorce. And they've lived together basically ever since.

I've always wondered, how is it between the two of them? How can they have complete trust in the other, considering how their relationship began? Maybe that's judgmental; I don't dwell on it. But if I was with a man who cheated <u>with</u> me, I'd always wonder if he'd also cheat <u>on</u> me.

Bottom line, though, I really think they're a better couple. They're really good for each other. She's certainly a better match for him than I was. But in some ways, I also think, you two just deserve each other.

There would never be full trust. And I couldn't do that. Certainly not at this age. I just don't have the energy to do that. I can't imagine not fully trusting whoever I was with. Maybe that's why I'm still single (laughs).

After my divorce, I wish I'd been smart enough to just take some time for myself. But I felt like we had led separate lives for so long that I was really excited to date again. I thought it'd be so fun to have somebody new, somebody who appreciates me. You know, all those things you think you're missing.

I got into a relationship with a guy that lasted about eighteen months. I knew it wasn't forever, but he was a lot of fun. We did a lot of things I'd never done before. He was really into football, and we traveled all over to watch professional football games. And we really had fun. It was different.

Eventually, I thought, This isn't really what I want.

After that first relationship, I took some time off and tried to figure out how to be alone. And that was one thing that was really important to me. I didn't really know how to be alone. I've never really been alone.

It was pretty rugged. Because I'd always been a full-time mom. I'd always had a husband. I had had family around me. And I remember, when those weekends would come, and I'd think, what am I going to do? My children were grown and had their own lives. Most of my friends were married. What would I do from Friday night until Monday morning?

And I remember feeling panicked. And really empty. There's just that readjustment of figuring out how you want to spend your hours.

Everything I read about being divorced over 50 said, Go find a church group. Do community service. And yet, in my heart I wasn't ready to do that. It was like the real sting of the divorce was delayed for me.

After the divorce, dating a lot, and finding new partners, that was all exciting. But finally at some point you have to feel the grief of your marriage ending. It's like a death. It's not what I planned. It's not what I'd envisioned myself doing in my fifties. And so, it's like, This sucks. This isn't where I pictured myself.

And I think that's how I spent that year or so. Really trying to figure out, What am I going to do? What am I going to do if there's not a man who comes in to rescue me this time?

I think until you actually go through the mourning process and come out the other side, you haven't done the work to actually be ready for somebody else. Or even for the next stage of life, if it's not with someone else.

I read a lot. I read Pema Chodron's book, When Things Fall Apart. And it said, Lean into the grief. That was the first time I'd ever heard that. And she said, Until you lean into the sharp edge of it, and accept it, it's not going to get better.

So I do remember a pretty dark year to eighteen months about three to four years after the divorce. I definitely went through it, if a bit out of order.

And I think coming out the other side really means that you're okay with whatever you choose. It might be looking for a new partner. Or you might just be excited to be alone.

In my case, I was just open to it if it happened. Awesome if it happens, but life is pretty damn good even if it doesn't.

I did get back to dating after that. I had long term relationships with a couple of different guys. But I never, in all of those eight years, met anybody that I thought, Oh yeah. This is who I could do two or three decades with.

In my twenties, there's no way I would have thought sex could be better when I'm "old." But it really is. There's a comfort level. You know who you are. And how you look. Face it, we've all been to the rodeo a time or two. We're comfortable, and it can be fun. Which it's supposed to be. Great, awesome, fun.

Though I haven't been with anyone for a while. But as I recall...(laughs)

I did some online dating. But after a while, I felt so past my divorce story. Typically, when you meet men, and they're freshly divorced, that's what they're still talking about. Understandably. I was too, at that point. Because that's your story. But after a while, that wasn't my story anymore.

Eight years after my divorce, I moved out of the U.S. I arrived without knowing anybody. Or speaking the language. I really had to get comfortable being alone. And navigating my way through a whole new culture. So it was good for me. It was really, really good for me to stand on my own two feet completely.

But I didn't make the move to look for a partner. The men here have a reputation for being so handsome and romantic. But I just thought, I need a little time out from it all. And I have great guy friends here, but those are business relationships. I don't cross that line.

I really haven't had a partner in these last four years. I dated a little bit. But nothing serious.

I gave myself a year to get a business going. And it turned out, women were reaching out to me to show them around where I was living. They were drawn to my story, and drawn to my area. So I realized there was a business here.

I love the people here, they are so generous and gracious. For me, I love sharing that. I want the people in my groups to be treated the way they would as a local.

It's not what I planned, but I'm in a really good place.

Afterward

So, what have we learned?

One message that comes through from the majority of the interviews is simply this: Divorce is hard, and it's painful, whether you wanted it or not. That pain is part of the process. Even if you're not necessarily grieving the loss of your marriage, you have suffered the death of your plan. Your vision for the future will not come to pass.

And there will be other struggles. Finances can get difficult, and lifestyles may be reduced. There may be issues with children, other family members, and friends. Loneliness will likely hit some newly divorced folks, with varying degrees of impact.

But there is a brighter future waiting. For many of the interviewees, life is so much better now. A few even celebrated their divorce. And though it was said in different ways, the point was clear: Their gray divorce allowed them to be who they want to be, and to look ahead optimistically to the next phase of their lives.

The interviewees' marriages ended for a variety of reasons, but there were some trends there as well. Communication – or more accurately, the lack of communication – was cited by multiple people. Money was another point of contention; in a few cases it was a spouse insisting they live above their means, and in others it was the breadwinner resenting the lack of contribution from the lower earner. Infidelity was the final straw in a few cases, though in others it was tolerated.

Sex was a problem in almost all the marriages. That certainly makes sense – caught in a deteriorating relationship, it's only natural that there'd be less and less intimacy. Several women said they basically endured it as part of their "wifely duties," in hopes of keeping their husbands happy, or of getting them to do household chores. Many interviewees reported absolutely no sex for the last several years of their marriages.

Most of the men interviewed had not yet begun a post-divorce sex life, and the one who had didn't offer any details about that aspect of his relationships.

However, many of the women who'd begun dating again were absolutely thrilled with their sex lives. Several would say they're currently having the best sex of their lives. Many reported strong libidos, oftentimes beyond what they remember from their teens and twenties. They felt more free to enjoy themselves now, unencumbered by pregnancy fears, worries about caring for small children, old fashioned morality, or the need to find a good provider/father for their children. More than one woman cited her complete comfort with her body now, unlike when she was younger.

Many of the women said they weren't interested in one-night-stands or friends-with-benefits situations; a couple of others have even surprised themselves with how boldly they are asserting their sexuality.

These interviews did provide some words of wisdom to anyone going through a divorce, or considering one. Among the more notable tips:

Know your finances. If you don't handle them, push yourself to find out what you and your spouse have (including retirement accounts), and what you owe.

Know your state's laws regarding divorce. Seek professional help if necessary to understand your rights and obligations.

If you know a divorce is coming (for example, you're waiting for your youngest to graduate high school), start making preparations. In addition to the financial and legal points made above, you need to get your mind and body right. Interviewees found great value from taking up yoga, meditation, and tai-chi.

Some people want to talk about their divorce with friends and family members, others do not. If you find it helpful, continue to reach out. But if you don't, you're entitled to set some boundaries. You're the one going through the difficult time – anyone who truly wants to help you will do it the way you want, not how they see fit.

And finally, though this book is aimed at the Over 50 reader who's either going through a Gray Divorce or is considering one, it became clear that it may also benefit that reader's children. Your kids, as they date and have romances and make choices about a future spouse, can learn from the mistakes we've all made – mistakes that come through so clearly in these interviews.

The first mistake was a poor choice of spouse. So many of the interviewees' marriages began under less than ideal circumstances, not even considering the ones that were pregnancy inspired. Multiple stories include comments about red flags that were ignored. Others admit to marrying for the wrong reasons, or to avoid returning to an abusive home, or simply because of wanting children. One woman was planning to break up with her boyfriend, but said yes when he proposed. Another laments accepting a proposal that was more like a business proposition.

And then, after the bad start, came the problems that were mentioned above: Communication, money, sex.

So if you've got young adult children, might it make sense to show them some of these stories? Couldn't reading about others' initial poor choices help young people make better decisions about a spouse? Wouldn't alerting them to the types of problems that arise later in marriages help them mitigate those issues in their own relationships?

I hope this book has been helpful, whether to make your Gray Divorce a little easier, or to help you decide about whether to go through one.

As always, here's looking ahead to a brighter future...

Made in the USA
Middletown, DE
10 December 2021

55123556R00073